STONE BY STONE

STONE ‑BY‑ STONE

The Magnificent History in New England's Stone Walls

ROBERT M. THORSON

WALKER & COMPANY ✸ NEW YORK

First published in the United States of America in 2002
by Walker Publishing Company, Inc.

Published simultaneously in Canada by Fitzhenry and Whiteside,
Markham, Ontario L3R 4T8

For information about permission to reproduce selections from this book, write to Permissions, Walker & Company, 435 Hudson Street, New York, New York 10014

Library of Congress Cataloging-in-Publication Data available upon request.
ISBN: 0-8027-1394-7

Visit Walker & Company's Web site at www.walkerbooks.com

Book design by M. J. DiMassi

Printed in the United States of America

2 4 6 8 10 9 7 5 3 1

TO MY FAMILY, FOR BEING PATIENT

Never tell me that not one star of all
That slip from heaven at night and softly fall
Has been picked up with stones to build a wall.

—from "A Star in a Stoneboat" by Robert Frost

CONTENTS

ဟေ

ACKNOWLEDGMENTS

My interest in stone walls began in 1984 when I moved from Alaska to the New England woodlands and had my first encounter with one. Its effect on my thinking—a mixture of surprise, incredulity, and curiosity—motivated me to pay attention to them as scientific objects instead of simply as artifacts. In 1990, while I held a fellowship in the history department at Yale University, sponsored by William Cronon and jointly funded by the Mellon Foundation, my interest evolved into a professional commitment to treat stone walls as landforms. Two years later, while I was a visiting scholar in geography at Dartmouth College, my commitment evolved into an actual investigation, half of which was carried out in the archive of its Baker Library, the other half in the foothills of New Hampshire's White Mountains during a field expedition sponsored by Earthwatch, and assisted by volunteers from around the country. The investigation finally turned into this book under the care of my agent, Lisa Adams, at the Garamond Agency, my editor, Jackie Johnson, and the rest of the staff of Walker & Company.

There are many others who helped along the way. At

Dartmouth, Robert Brackenridge sponsored my appointment, Jere Daniel introduced me to the enigmatic photographer Wallace Nutting, and Jeff Hawkins helped me calculate the metabolic rate of its football team. Gordon Whitney of Harvard Forest made available its unpublished archive of maps, and helped me hone my arguments more sharply. Jack Larkin of Old Sturbridge Village, Massachusetts, and Esther Morn Swift of the Billings Farm Museum in Woodstock, Vermont, provided unpublished data on land-use patterns and helped critique my ideas. David Porier of the Connecticut State Historical Commission shared many of his sources.

At the University of Connecticut, my colleagues Jamie Eves, Harold Spencer, and Randall Steinen reviewed the manuscript for errors in their respective disciplines of history, art, and science. Robert Gradie and Kevin McBride helped introduce me to stone walls on early field trips. Carol Davidge, Ray Joesten, Marylin Nelson, Sam Pickering, and Suzie Staubach encouraged me through it all. I appreciate the assistance of my graduate students, especially Robert Cless, Dan Forrest, and Gregory Brick.

At home, I had the support of my family, particularly Kristine Hoy Thorson, who convinced me that words really do matter, and my sons, Tyler and Kevin, whose habit of looking for gems in our crushed-stone driveway convinced me that stones were interesting to almost everyone. I was also inspired by my daughter Katrina, whose favorite playscape is our most tumbled-down wall.

Most important, I want to thank Howard Russell, Susan Allport, David Foster, William Cronon, Kevin Gardner, David Leveson, J. B. Jackson, Roderick Nash, Wendell Berry,

Chet and Maureen Raymo, and Annie Dillard for sharing their ideas through their books. Without access to them, *Stone by Stone* would be little more than a chain of geoarchaeological inferences.

STONE BY STONE

❧

A tumbled woodland wall.

INTRODUCTION

ABANDONED STONE WALLS ARE THE SIGNATURES OF RURAL New England. Crisscrossing the parks, suburbs, and farms of nearly every village and town, they are relics of a vanished agricultural civilization that once flourished in hillside farming communities. In 1939, the mining engineer Oliver Bowles, using data from an 1872 Department of Agriculture report on fences, estimated that there were approximately 240,000 miles of stone walls in New England.[1] That's longer than the U.S. coastline, or even the distance to the Moon at perigee. The mass of stone used in those walls is greater than that from all the remaining ancient monuments put together.

There are old stone walls elsewhere, but only in New England do they rise above the level of architectural ornaments to the status of landforms. Kentucky has its caves, Florida its coral reefs, Louisiana its bayous, Arizona its arroyos, Washington its volcanoes, Minnesota its lakes, and New England its stone walls. The landscape would simply not be the same without them.

Conventional histories correctly describe how New England's stone walls were built by farmers who patiently cleared glacier-dropped stones from their fields. But history alone cannot account for the magnitude of the phenomenon, or for their structure—thick, low, and crudely stacked. To understand the archetypal stone walls in New England—primitive, mortar-free, and "tossed" rather than carefully laid—one must turn to the techniques of the natural sciences, in which observation, induction, and analysis carry more weight than the quasimythic tales of early America.

The story of stone walls is a very old one, and is appropriately told by a geologist, whose job it is to reconstruct the history of the Earth. The emergence and decay of New England's stone walls falls under the domain of geoarchaeology, a subdiscipline whose goal is to interpret human artifacts within a broader geological perspective. Consider this book a geoarchaeological study of stone walls, the first of its kind.

๑๑

STONE WALLS LIE AT THE INTERSECTION OF SCIENCE AND history, which became woven together during the transformation of wilderness into family farms, and have been part of the same fabric ever since. Although the New England upland has many old, dilapidated walls, stones were not always abundant in the region.

The raw material from which the stones were made began as mud from oceans, here and there, that have long since vanished. For example, much of central New England once lay in a narrowing sea that disappeared completely when North America, Africa, and Europe merged as part of a supercontinent called Pangaea. Just before the continents separated, this material was deeply buried, squeezed, and sheared into a beautifully swirled lump of hot rock. Over time, it cooled, hardened, decompressed, and rose up to become hard bedrock, mantled by deep, clay-rich, pinkish-yellow, less fertile soils, and covered mostly by forest.

New England did not become stony until the Laurentide Ice Sheet invaded the region from central Canada fifteen to thirty thousand years ago. It stripped away the last of these ancient soils, scouring the land down to its bedrock, lifting up billions of stone slabs and scattering them across the region. It also left behind "till," a hardpan soil that was, almost single-handedly, responsible for the success of the grazing economy in New England, which provided its beef, bacon, and butter. As the lush, temperate, deciduous forest returned, however, natural processes within the soil buried most of the stones beneath the thick, organic, loamy soil that was so often discovered by pioneering settlers. The stones were there, but most were hidden from sight.

Native American tribes—Iroquois, Mohegan, Pequot, Penobscot, Nipmuck and Wampanuag, and others, as well as their ancestors—became an important part of the forest ecosystem throughout northeastern North America during the epoch after deglaciation. They settled intensively in the coastal lowlands and large river valleys and, during the last thousand years, cultivated crops. But their resident populations remained negligible on the upland terrain, where, to the south, old-growth forests of maple, oak, hemlock, hickory, and pine flourished, and to the north, birch, maple, spruce, and beech, in spite of frequent disturbance by wind storms and fire. Native hunting parties trod lightly on the forest floor, leaving the stones untouched and the soils thickening quietly and ceaselessly. This was not the case on the other side of the Atlantic, where the Neolithic ancestors of the English had been tilling and grazing upland soils for millennia.

New England upland soils continued to thicken during early European settlement of the region, which began with the arrival of the Pilgrims at Plymouth, Massachusetts, in 1620. Agricultural fields of the original colonies and "plantations" were generally located in stone-free coastal lowlands and in broad river valleys. These settlements were initially somewhat communal; farmers shared common pastures and tillage fields during the day, and retreated to the protection of densely occupied villages at night. Private property did exist, but it lay within larger, community-managed parcels on floodplains. The upland remained a dangerous, largely unoccupied place to the settlers until lingering hostilities between the colonists and the Native Americans lessened with the end of the French and Indian Wars in the mid–eighteenth century. It was during this phase that early stone walls were constructed, usually near villages and often with stone taken from quarries and slopes rather than from fields; meanwhile, the stones of the interior remained hidden beneath the old-growth forests and a deepening, rich soil.

But during the last half century before the American Revolution, thousands of freedom-seeking sons and daughters—formerly confined in increasingly crowded ancestral villages like Boston, Hartford, Providence, New Haven, and Portland (once called Falmouth)—began to establish pioneering settlements in the thickly wooded interior. By that time land-use practices had already shifted to a more broadly distributed pattern of independent, self-sufficient, freeholding farmers. The ideological transition toward individual liberty and private property spread a patchwork of private farms over the rich soils of the uplands, each of which required well-defined boundaries and plenty of fencing.

The rapid spread of farms across the uplands coincided with the culminating century of the "Little Ice Age," a climatic epoch that had begun about A.D. 1300 and ended in the late nineteenth century. This marked the beginning of the present phase of climatic warming; colonial times were colder times. As pioneers cleared the forests, there was initially plenty of wood for heating and fencing, and there were not that many stones, except in the worst places. But soon after deforestation, especially on tillage land, the soil became much more exposed to winter cold, causing it to freeze deeply before each inevitable spring thaw. The deep freezing greatly accelerated the process of frost heaving, in which stones are incrementally lifted through the finer-grained soil, toward the surface. When spring rains and snowmelt came, the water couldn't infiltrate as easily as through unfrozen, forested soil, forcing it to flow over the surface with erosive force, removing the loam and concentrating the stone. The clearing of stones from pastures and fields became an annual chore for at least a generation.

In colonial and early America, farmers used their fences to pen animals for the strategic dropping of manure and to separate livestock and crops. Subdivision of land within families added even more boundaries. Thousands of fence lines became magnets for the stone refuse that would otherwise have ended up in piles. Stones were often lugged to field side by hand and tossed one upon the other. More commonly, a load of stone was skidded to the edge of the field on a stout wooden sled pulled by a team of oxen. The large boulders were rolled into position; smaller stones were tossed above and between them. As the stone accumulated, primitive "tossed" walls began to rise up out of the weeds, replacing the lower tiers of wooden fences.

During the early decades of the eighteenth century, many primitive walls were rebuilt into more architecturally pleasing forms, especially on prosperous farms and estates. This era of agricultural improvement coincided with a time when farm populations were rising and when a surplus of labor was available. It also coincided with a time when the stone supply was increasing relative to the wood supply. With cash, labor, and a copious supply of stone already in place, hundreds of thousands of walls were built and rebuilt throughout the region by farmers, hired labor, the unemployed, and slaves.

ৣৣ

THE AUTHENTIC EARLY STONE WALLS OF NEW ENGLAND served many purposes. A small few were tall enough and strong enough to qualify as legal fences. Many others were expedient boundary markers separating private lands, No Trespassing signs written in stone. A few were ornaments, built for aesthetic purposes or to display wealth. But almost every wall also served a more fundamental, arguably higher purpose: to hold the waste stone that once littered farm fields. However tidy well-built walls might appear, most functioned originally as linear landfills, built to hold nonbiodegradable agricultural refuse.

Nearly every attribute of authentic backwoods walls is consistent with this claim. For example, the size of an enclosed field was often determined by the number of walls required to hold the stone that was picked up from it. The height of most walls—thigh high—was governed more by the ergonomics of lifting and tossing stone than by the mandate of fencing. The simple, inward-slanting, internal structure of most walls was a "least-work" trade-off between the investment of energy required to build the wall and its long-term stability.

Stone walls not only transformed waste into something useful, they arguably "improved" the local wildlife habitat with respect to diversity. Prior to wall construction, the dry-land habitats of cliffs and ledges were much more restricted in New England; animals and plants that had adapted to such terrain now had a greater chance to survive because stone walls and stone ledges offered similar opportunities.

Walls have also influenced the terrain directly. Hilltop walls forced the rain toward different streams. Lowland walls impounded many small wetlands, caused the buildup of soil on slopes, and acted as underground drains on floodplains. Stone walls are so tightly enmeshed with streams, slopes, and soils that the distinction between wall and nonwall is often unclear.

౿౿

PAYING CLOSER ATTENTION TO STONE WALLS FROM A SCIENTIFIC perspective helps deconstruct some pervasive historic myths. First is the notion that New England pioneers cleared a rocky wasteland in order to create their farms. In reality, upland New England farms were then, and remained at all times provided they were treated with care, largely fertile until they were abandoned for cultural and technological reasons. Most of the stone that found its way into walls was a delayed and inadvertent consequence of deforestation. Like the local extinction of bears, wolves, and cougars, stony soils were an unavoidable environmental consequence of wilderness conversion.

Second, there is the mistaken impression that stone walls are primarily a colonial phenomenon. They are not. Although walls were being built from the time of the first settlement to the end of the pioneering stage, most were built in the half century between the end of the American Revolution and the construction of the first railroads. Early colonial settlements were in river and coastal lowlands, which were usually underlain by thick deposits of glacial sand and mud devoid of stone except on rocky headlands. There are indeed many colonial-era stone walls in the ancient towns of Rhode Island, eastern Massachusetts, and southern Connecticut. But even in those regions, most old walls were built later.

Finally, most stone walls were never stand-alone fences, intentionally built to separate livestock and crops or one neighbor from another. Nearly all needed some help from wood, then later wire, to accomplish this task. Fences created the walls, rather than the other way around.

Knowing more about stone walls allows one to appreciate them—and the landscape they embellish—more keenly. With very little effort, you can also become a more discriminating admirer of stone walls. Initially, you will see walls where you might not have noticed them before. Later, you will see more conspicuous differences among walls and stones. Finally, you will discern subtle clues to a wall's construction and its history, both natural and human.

To know New England well, one must know its stone walls. Forged at scorching temperatures deep within the Earth and brought to the region by huge glaciers, each stone is the result of both fire and ice. Today's stone walls continue to be transformed, largely by biological processes. Bacteria tarnish them. Lichens dissolve them. Vines penetrate and loosen their stones. Trees, blown down during hurricanes, knock large gaps in walls, as though taking bites of the earth. Left untended, every wall will come apart, tumble to the ground, disperse over acres of soil, and be buried by the encroaching vegetation. Although inanimate, stone walls have an important story to tell. They give us a clock by which we can judge the passage of almost unimaginable time.

1

ENGLAND AND NEW ENGLAND, COMMON GROUND

EUROPEAN SETTLEMENT OF NEW ENGLAND BEGAN not in 1620 when the Pilgrims dropped anchor in Cape Cod Bay, but in 1607, the same year the Jamestown Colony was established in Virginia.[1] The initial attempt at a permanent New England settlement—called the North Virginia Company—took place at Sagadahoc, Maine, on the inner coast north of what is now Portland. There the climate was rigorous; winters were especially difficult. The terrain was rocky, with plentiful bedrock ledges, steep bluffs, stony soils, narrow marshes, and streams. Everyone left within a year. The Sagadahoc settlement had failed, perhaps because its landscape was too cold and hard, too different from that of the mother country, England.

The English returned to the region in 1620, landing much farther to the south, near Plymouth, in what is now southeastern Massachusetts. This group of religious dissidents, later known as the Pilgrims, disembarked the *Mayflower* to encounter terrain less rocky than that in Maine and a climate less hostile to survival. Times were hard, but the Pilgrims persisted. They proved that life north of the Virginia colonies was possible, if only barely.

**Map showing earliest
New England settlements.**

A decade later, the third English migration to New England aimed for the middle ground between Sagadahoc and Cape Cod. This group, which formed the Massachusetts Bay Colony, struck near Boston, naming it after a village in the old country. Unlike the adventurers and separatists who preceded them, these Puritans were more typical of the contemporary English middle class, being better educated, involved in more skilled professions, and having come in greater numbers primarily to escape religious intolerance. Using maps made by Captain John Smith, they chose their landfall near Boston wisely, founding what has since become the economic and cultural center of New England.

The terrain near Boston was more yielding than that of Maine, yet firmer than that of Plymouth, which was located on the shore of Cape Cod Bay and had a greater abundance of shifting, sandy, droughty soils. This middle ground had wide, navigable, freshwater rivers; deep harbors; sheltered bays; and stable shorelines. Broad salt marshes were nurseries for fisheries and there were abundant freshwater springs. Soils were fertile and loamy, yet light enough to be grubbed free of roots and worked with handheld shovels and hoes; this was especially true in places previously cleared by the Woodland Indians for their crops of corn, beans, and gourds. Marsh hay—a mixture of reeds, sedge, and grass that grew naturally near high tide—was available for cattle fodder, which was essential for survival. Whitefish, alewives, lobsters, horseshoe crabs, kelp, and whatever else washed ashore could fertilize cereal grains, especially wheat and corn. The proximity to the sea moderated the bitter cold of winter, and lessened summer drought. The landscape was almost ideal. The climate, though seasonally cold, was healthful.

Within a century, the Massachusetts Bay Colony had become so successful that it expanded northward to engulf the failed colony of Sagadahoc, and southward to include Plymouth Plantation. The success of the Massachusetts Bay Colony was due largely to the industry of its inhabitants, who skillfully exploited the natural resources along New England's inner coast, but also to the natural affinity the English had for the land bordering the Massachusetts Bay Colony. Indeed, the English felt at home, naming their communities—Cambridge, Dartmouth, Ipswich, and Dorchester—after similar places on the other side of the Atlantic.

In fact, England and New England had similar landscapes and climates because both lands had a similar geologic history. Millions of years ago, in the Paleozoic era Old World and New World, motherland and daughterland were formed within the same mountain range near the center of the ancient continent Pangaea. Ever since then, they have been tied to the same geological fate.[2]

To understand why the land of New England is so similar to that of Old England, and how the similar fieldstones on opposite sides of the Atlantic were created practically within the same foundry, it is necessary to go back to the inception of earthly time, 4.6 billion years ago. The story that follows explains why there are so many stones, why they are so widely distributed, and why they were perfectly shaped for human handling.

ᴐᴑ

TO THE PURITANS, HELL WAS A PLACE OF ETERNAL DAMNATION, hot, dark, and sulfurous. However, in geologic terms, hell is not a place but a time. The Hadean Eon, spanning the first half billion years of Earth's history, was a protracted interval of volcanic fury that took place while the planet was still accumulating as a collection of fragments from asteroids and comets, and dust and gas from exploded planets.

During the Hadean Eon (an eon is a span of time long enough to hold eras and epochs), the heat released by intense asteroid bombardment combined with the heat released by radioactive decay to melt the planet. Molten lava oozed up to the surface, forming a bubbling ocean of red-hot liquid that quickly hardened into basalt, a black rock that formed Earth's most primitive crust. Meanwhile, heavier metallic components seeped downward, forming its core, a mass of iron that is solid metal at the center but liquid in the outer core. Earth's rotation (spinning more rapidly than now) caused swirling motions within the outer core, which produced the planet's magnetic field, and thus protected the early Earth from the sun's intense ionizing radiation.

Between the Earth's core and its crust lies its mantle, an enormous region of warm, dense, dark-greenish rock that is solid, but malleable enough to flow and be stretched. The continents are made of the lightest of Earth's solid layers. From its hot, molten origin, Earth became a solid but squishy glob of soft rock that rotated rapidly on its tilted axis, perhaps up to five hundred days per year, while wobbling like a top.

As Earth's interior melted, volatile gases boiled up and created an atmosphere rich in noxious substances. Nitrogen, carbon dioxide, and water vapor were heavy enough to be retained by Earth's gravity, whereas lighter gases such as helium were mostly lost to space. When the atmosphere first formed, Earth's crust was as hot as a broiler, prohibiting the condensation of the water at or near its surface. Any drops that fell to the surface quickly flashed to a cloud of steam, then back to vapor. Therefore, all the Earth's water was held in high clouds so dense and thick that they blocked out the sunlight completely.

At that point, Earth's lava surface was perpetually dark and parching hot. What dim light there was came from the orange-hot glow of flowing lava; the constant "heat" lightning from distant clouds; and the yellow-green flashes of meteorites, which until about 3.8 billion years ago streaked through Earth's carbon-rich sky by the billions.

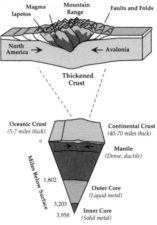

Structure of the Earth

Diagram of interior Earth structure (bottom) and a typical collisional mountain range (top).

Eventually, the Earth cooled down. The shroud of vapor condensed into mist, then mist to droplets, and droplets became drops. Rain began to fall, not just for a few hours or a few days, but for thousands of years, until the original atmosphere had rained itself dry. Torrents of water drenched the now solidified lava that covered the entire planet. Rivulets of fresh water—not yet stained by salts, clays, and dissolved organic compounds—flowed noisily in the darkness, seeking the low places. First, pools were formed, then ponds, lakes, and finally a global ocean. Simultaneously, the sky gradually brightened, as though part of a long, drawn-out dawn, thousands of years in the making. One day, the first gleaming ray of sunlight broke through the thinning clouds to strike an azure ocean so young that it was not yet salty, and so expansive that hardly any dry land existed.

As the Earth cooled further, lingering volcanism produced masses of molten rock called magma that were lighter in weight, lighter in color, and richer in silica than Earth's earlier, heavier, more primitive magmas that produced only basalt. These lighter-weight masses of molten rock cooled to make lighter-colored rocks similar to granite, which floated slightly higher above the mantle than their basaltic counterparts. Over time, blotches of granite crust coalesced like flotsam on a stream, fusing into proto-continents that were light enough to float above the level of the sea, thus making dry land.

At some point in Earth's cooling history, the outermost fifty miles or so—equivalent to the thickness of the skin on a peach—became a rigid shell called the lithosphere. Because the lithosphere lay above a much thicker, softer, still-swirling mantle, it broke up into giant tectonic plates, which glided slowly over the surface, carrying the continents along for the ride. No longer a hot, dark, crater-blemished, quiet lump of debris gathered by gravity from the solar system, Earth had been transformed into a machine, powered by the heat from its interior, radiation from the sun, and the angular momentum of its planetary spin. The tectonic plates moved independently, like juggernauts, making mountains where they collided, ocean basins where they separated, and enormous valleys where they slid against one another.

Earth's atmosphere traveled quickly over the oceans, producing wind and waves, and the ocean's sluggish movement over its crust produced tides and currents. Wind storms, thunder, waves, torrents of running water, earthquakes, and volcanic explosions were the sounds of Earth's vital fluids moving about, yet there wasn't a single creature alive to hear them.

Life began about four billion years ago, probably on some hot, briny, pitch-black, undersea volcanic vent. From that remote bacterial beginning, the evolution of life commenced. For most of Earth history, however, life would remain simple and confined beneath the sea. Only after ninety percent of Earth history had passed would creatures evolve legs and become strong enough to live on land. It was during this life transition—from oceanic slime to terrestrial animals—that the raw material for the stones of New England began to form.

This inception took place in the Iapetos Ocean, the precursor to the Atlantic, which occupied roughly the same place; Iapetos was the mythological father of Atlas, for whom the Atlantic is named. The Iapetos Ocean disappeared as the ancient landmasses of Africa, Europe, and North America converged upon each other during the formation of Pangaea. The former ocean's water could easily flow elsewhere on Earth. But the solid material that had lain between the three continents—abyssal marine mud, plankton oozes, volcanic islands, old shorelines, limy reefs, small blocks of crust, and other earthly flotsam—was scraped off the floor of the ocean and added to the edge of North America, which at that time lay much farther south, near the equator.

The culmination of this continent-to-continent collision occurred about three hundred million years ago, shortly before the dinosaurs began to rule the planet. Called the

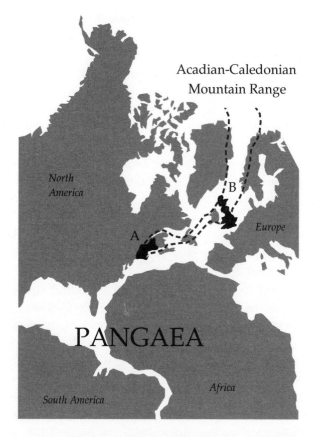

*Map of Pangaea showing New England (A) and
Old England (B).*

Acadian Orogeny in New England and the Caledonian
Orogeny in Britain, it produced a mountain range that
traced a seam through the center of Pangaea, where the
continents had been stitched together. Indeed, the fjord-
torn mountains of Norway shared the same bedrock with
Greenland; the central Appalachians were attached to West

Africa. The lands in between—New England, maritime Canada, and Britain—were pressed tightly together during the three-way collision.

A small fragment of continental crust geologists call Avalonia, caught up in this collision, has since broken into separate pieces. One now lies beneath southeastern England, another beneath southeastern New England. On the other side of the collision lay what is called the Greenville Terrane, which later broke up as well; its rocks form the northwestern part of the British Isles, including Scotland, and the northwestern edge of New England from western Connecticut to western Maine. Most of what lies between—Ireland, central England, and Wales on one side of the Atlantic and most of central New England on the other— was made from the mud and clay of the Iapetos Ocean.

Any land caught in the collision zone and squeezed horizontally by the relentless tectonic stresses was also thrust vertically upward, producing a mountain range so massive that it couldn't be supported by the strength of the Earth's crust alone. Hence, the vast bulk of the mountain range, extending from Florida to northern Norway, sank deeply into the softer mantle of the Earth, in places as much as twenty miles. Essentially, only the upper part of the mountain chain remained above the ocean while most of it lay well below sea level, as though it were an enormous stone iceberg. (Something similar is happening in the Himalayas today, where the ongoing collision between India and Asia has produced a range of mountains made by materials scraped off the floor of a disappeared ocean. The Himalayas above sea level today are but a small fraction of their total mass underground.)

It was in the root of the "Acadian Mountains," whose

eroded stubs are now the northern Appalachians, that New England's stones were created ten to twenty miles straight down. A dry, hot mélange of minerals baked slowly within the Earth, at a depth more than five times that of the deepest mine. Temperatures sometimes exceeded that of flowing lava. Pressures were thousands of times greater than those above ground. Briny waters were forced out of pore spaces as they squeezed shut, carrying with them gold, silver, mercury, and other precious metals dissolved in boiling fluids. Carbon, nitrogen, hydrogen, and other lighter, volatile elements that had originally been extracted from the Earth's atmosphere by biological processes and sunk to the ocean floor burned away and were vented back to the skies. Primary rock-forming elements—silicon, oxygen, aluminum, calcium, sodium, iron, potassium, magnesium—were left behind and forced to recombine into new minerals that were stable under these new conditions. Clay cooked to mica, grit into quartz. Enormous masses of rock the size of Rhode Island and rendered soft by the heat stretched and bent like taffy, folding into each other, miles below the surface.

Over time, the once mundane materials of the former Iapetos Ocean—mud, muddy sand, sandy mud, sand— were transformed into the beautiful banded rocks visible over most of New England today. Some of these rocks are layered like a cake. Others resemble succotash, with clots of crystals. Some of the manufactured minerals would become vital to early Yankee industry—pink feldspar for ceramics, smoky quartz for glass, brown garnets for abrasives, white barite for paint thickener, bronze sheets of mica for furnace windows, green talc for lubricants, gray veins of graphite for pencil lead, and black specks of iron oxide for steel. Colonial mining was a colorful, and locally successful, business.

ᴕᴕ

PANGAEA WAS DESTINED TO FALL APART. THE THICKENED crust acted like a skullcap, trapping the heat that is always escaping from the Earth's interior. As the upper mantle warmed beneath Pangaea, it expanded slightly, lifting the supercontinent upward and producing a bulge more than a mile high. The continent stretched, thinned, and finally broke, similar to the way the top of a loaf of bread sometimes splits. The uplift and rupture of Pangaea formed a volcanic rift zone that ran from south to north, from Georgia to Greenland.

Along the crest of the rift zone were long basins (similar to those of California's Death Valley, Jordan's Dead Sea, and Africa's Lake Victoria), each of which subsided as the crust pulled apart. Initially, this occurred slowly enough for the rivers draining from the highlands to be able to keep the widening basins filled with sediment, crossing them with broad, meandering channels. But eventually the subsidence along bordering faults was so rapid that deep, narrow lakes were created. Sediment being shed from the eroding highlands poured into these lakes. On several occasions, the rift fractures penetrated so deeply that they tapped into pools of basaltic magma, which gushed upward along fissures to form lava lakes up to several hundred feet deep and tens of miles long. Such lava flows, after solidifying and being tipped to the side, later became known as traprock ridges.

The pebbles, sand, mud, and lava flows of the rift basin

were deposited about 225 to 170 million years ago, making them Late Triassic to Early Jurassic in age. After being deposited, these sediments kept on subsiding until they were buried at least five miles deep, enough to convert the sandy, pebbly sediment into rocks, but not so deep as to convert them into the much harder, crystalline rocks more common in the highlands. Sedimentary rocks are among the softest rocks of New England. Most of this bedrock was tinted by iron in a strongly monsoon climate to a beautiful reddish-brown color, called *colorado* in Spanish. Early colonists called it freestone because it was so easy to quarry. Nineteenth-century architects called it brownstone, and used it to construct thousands of urban buildings throughout the northeast. Within this brownstone rock—whether in road cuts, quarries, or buildings—are abundant fossils of early Mesozoic life, notably dinosaurs and the primitive lakeshore vegetation they prowled through.

In New England, the rift zone runs from New Haven, Connecticut, to near Hanover, New Hampshire, and is now drained by the Connecticut River, whose famous, flat "interval" lands—Wethersfield, Hartford, Windsor, Springfield, Holyoke, Deerfield, Brattleboro—were once ancient, equatorial, alkaline lakes. These interval lands are broad and low today, not because their basins are still subsiding, but because their rift-basin sediment, being softer than the rock of adjacent highlands, has been more deeply eroded. Without rifting, there would have been no Atlantic Ocean for the British to cross on their journey to North America. Nor would there have been the Connecticut River Valley, the portal through which most of the western interior of New England was settled.

ဟ၁

THE FINAL RUPTURE OF PANGAEA TOOK PLACE BETWEEN what is now Rhode Island and northwest Africa, near Morocco. Old England and New England began to separate like two sides of an eggshell being cracked above a bowl, moving inexorably away from each other at the rate a human fingernail grows each year. (Somewhere south of modern Iceland, in the middle of the Atlantic, is a line of undersea volcanoes where the rift zone is active today, although it was not discovered until the use of submarine sonar technology in the mid–twentieth century. This undersea rift marks the line where England and New England last parted company, 200 million years ago.)

Even after the continents pulled apart, England and New England continued to have similarities. Both lay on the passive sides of their respective continents, where they would escape later tectonic collisions. Never again would either be thrust up into mountains along an "active" plate margin, such as those on the western sides of North and South America. England now lies near the middle of the European Plate; New England now lies near the center of the North American Plate. Nevertheless, both are still being stretched and strained by plate motions that can occasionally produce moderately strong earthquakes. William Bradford, governor of Plymouth Plantation, described one of New England's most violent events, which occurred in June of 1638.

> *This year, aboute the 1. Or 2. of June was a*
> *great and fearfull earthquake ... It came with*
> *a rumbling noyse, or low murmure, like unto*
> *remoate thunder; it came from the norward*

and passed southward. As the noyse aproched
nerer, they earth begane to shake . . . and the
earth shooke with that violence as [women]
could not stand without catching hould of the
posts and pails that stood next them. . . . So
powerfull is the mighty hand of the Lord, as to
make both the earth and sea to shake and the
mountaines to tremble before him, when he
pleases; and who can stay his hand?[3]

The Atlantic Ocean kept widening as England and New England moved away from the hot oceanic rift between them. The crust beneath both lands stabilized and cooled. As it became cooler, the crust beneath both lands contracted, making it more dense, which allowed it to sink lower into the mantle. Both lands became lower with every passing epoch.

England and New England kept drifting into similar midlatitude, maritime climates. Frequent rains, forest vegetation, thick clay-rich soils, and perennial streams ensured that an endless supply of sand and mud was carried by rivers into the sea. Their rugged highlands on separate sides of the Atlantic eroded—a gradual process that continues to lower the landscape, even today. Coastal plains developed on the stabilized continental margins, accumulating layer by layer from sediment shed from continental interiors. Among these coastal-plain sediments in England and New England are soft Cretaceous rocks—named for the chalk cliffs of Dover—that are also exposed from the island of Nantucket to New Jersey. After erosion over a period of 250 hundred million years, most of Old and New England had been reduced to low sur-

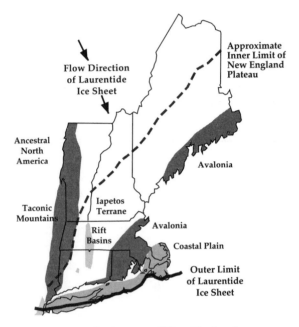

**Approximate
Inner Limit of
New England
Plateau**

**Flow Direction
of Laurentide
Ice Sheet**

**Ancestral
North
America**

Avalonia

**Taconic
Mountains**

**Iapetos
Terrane**

**Rift
Basins**

Avalonia

Coastal Plain

**Outer Limit
of Laurentide
Ice Sheet**

A geologic map of New England.

faces that rose gradually inland from their respective coastal plains.

Within the last few million years, however, these ancient erosion surfaces were gently lifted above the level of the sea, a process that is especially evident on the American side, where a broad uplift occurred. In response, all of the important New England rivers—the Penobscot, the Kennebec, the Saco, the Merrimack, the Charles, the Blackstone, the Thames, the Connecticut, the Housatonic, and the Hudson—and their countless tributaries cut deeply downward into the broader, less

rugged, preexisting valleys. As a result, the older landscape was stranded as a broad, irregular plateau, typically
standing two hundred feet or more above the streams of
today.

This undulating ancient surface is called the New
England Plateau.[4] Eroded from the roots of old mountains,
uplifted, and heavily glaciated, it was to become the agricultural and industrial heartland of the region in the late
eighteenth and early nineteenth centuries. Upon its upper
surface lay fertile fields and pastures surrounded by tens of
thousands of stone walls. Cut below this surface was a network of clean, free-flowing streams, across which were
thousands of dams and mills that powered Yankee industry. Both aspects of the landscape were a consequence of
a geological history that produced nearly identical results
on opposite sides of the Atlantic.

∾

THE HISTORY SHARED BY MOTHERLAND AND DAUGHTERLAND
didn't stop with the formation of their inland plateaus. It
continued with the intense glaciation of the last 2 million
years, a phenomenon that created stony landscapes in the
Old and New Worlds, and which helped cut coastal valleys
in both lands well below sea level. In England, the south-
moving ice sheets stopped just short of London, whereas
in New England the ice sheets stopped at the chain of islands from Nantucket, Massachusetts, to Staten Island,
New York. Broadly speaking, the Thames River in London, England, and the Thames River in New London,
Connecticut, have similar natural histories. Both have been
flooded by the rising level of the sea within the last fifteen
thousand years, which rose as the ice sheets melted.

Deepwater estuaries and flanking salt marshes in both lands result from the same basic causes.

In terms of the natural scenery, a journey from the English Lake District, near the border with Scotland, to the cliffs of Dover, opposite France, resembles one from the White Mountains of New Hampshire to Chatham, Cape Cod. Perhaps it is no coincidence that the failure of the colony at Sagadahoc, Maine, and the limited success of Plymouth Plantation took place where the geology differed most from that of England. The Puritan adventurers, at least in their settlement patterns, were more conservative than more conventional histories would suggest.

2

MAKING THE STONE

TONE, RATHER THAN ORE, HAS ALWAYS BEEN THE primary mineral resource in New England.[1] Even at the outset, when buildings were made of mud wattle and thatched with grass, stone was used for chimneys, sills, building foundations, and pathways. Beginning in the late 1600s, stone also was used for grave markers, which were in heavy demand during the earliest years of European colonization when the mortality rate among children was high. New England stone, besides being nearly ubiquitous, was fireproof, hard, durable, and came in convenient-size slabs. They would have been quite familiar to early colonists, who had seen plenty like them in the old country, especially north of London.

The attributes of New England stones are a legacy of the region's geological history, one that involved both fire and ice. Fire—conditions hot enough to melt glass under normal pressures—burned deep in the roots of the Acadian Mountains, in the center of Pangaea. It was responsible for making the hard, crystalline bedrock from which the fieldstones would later be broken. Ice—an Antarctic-size glacier that scraped its way over New England—invaded the region from the hinterlands of cen-

***Five kinds of metamorphic rocks (from left to right:
gneiss, schist, granite, slate, and basalt).***

tral Canada. Glaciation was responsible for prying the
slabs out of the bedrock; shaping them with grinding,
banging, crushing, tumbling, and scratching actions; and
scattering them over the landscape, ensuring that nearly
every farmer's field had its fair share.

New England stone was forged at high temperature
and pressure, deep within the Earth. It was transformed, or
"metamorphosed," from a softer, raw material without ever
melting completely. Most of the metamorphic rock in the
region is conspicuously layered, a characteristic called foliation, which sometimes appears similar to the layers of
sedimentary rock. However, foliation is caused by the gradual growth during metamorphism of platy crystals, especially those made of mica (and quartz), which align them-

selves as they grow. Foliation can also be produced when shearing motions take place deep in the crust as masses of rock squeeze past one another.

Although a piece of marble plucked from a Berkshire quarry started out as limy mud, most other metamorphic rocks come from common silicate materials and are classified by the amount of change they have suffered. Slate, shiny and tightly foliated, is only slightly transformed, and thus is quite weak, like unfired pottery. The crystals in schist are larger, visible to the naked eye, and are aligned like the grain of wood, but the rock is not conspicuously banded. Gneiss, a rock with very distinct banding, usually of light and dark layers, forms when the atoms of quasi-melted minerals break down chemically, segregating into visible layers, each with its own mineralogy. Migmatite, being partially molten, is ultrametamorphosed. Quartzite, the strongest rock in New England, is usually made from sandstone that was baked at a high temperature, as though it were fired in a kiln.

In some places, however, especially in the deepest mountain roots, the original masses of rock melted completely, forming magma of granite composition. This stiff, puddinglike liquid later crystallized into hard, light-colored, often black-speckled igneous rocks. (Rocks that cool from a melt are termed "igneous rocks.") Some of the granite magma squirted through fractures of host rock, producing light-colored veins. But the majority of magma rose slowly upward through the Earth's outer crust as giant blobs that solidified underground in city-size masses called batholiths. Granite is usually stronger than other metamorphic rock because it doesn't have a "grain"; it tends to break into chunks rather than slabs. The spine of mountains in western New England—the Berkshires, the White Mountains, the Presidential Range, the Katahdin Range—stands high because the granite blobs frozen beneath them are thick and strong.

Vertical fissures that penetrated deep into the crust along the rift zone sometimes tapped into darker, heavier magma. This magma froze in the fissures and between rock layers, forming resistant dikes and sills of black basalt, which typically rusts to an orange-tinted olive color; the Palisades along the Lower Hudson River is a good example of basalt sill that solidified underground. Usually this magma remained liquid, reached the surface, and flowed over the land as streams of lava, gathering into broad sheets before hardening into solid rock. These frozen sheets of lava, or traprock ridges, form highlands in the Connecticut River Valley, between New Haven, Connecticut, and Holyoke, Massachusetts. They stand high because they are hard. They're asymmetric because they are tilted.

Not all of New England's rocks are hard metamorphic rocks (slate, schist, gneiss, quartzite, or migmatite) or igneous rocks (granite and basalt). Sedimentary rocks—those composed of particles that are not baked or melted enough to qualify as metamorphic in origin—and very weakly metamorphosed rocks called greenschist rocks (for their dusky green color) are also quite common, especially in the triangle of land between Boston, New Bedford, and Providence, and in northern Maine. Weak metamorphic rocks are also abundant in the Green Mountains of Vermont, the Berkshires of western Massachusetts and Connecticut, and the Taconics of New York east of the Hudson River. These rocks are not only conspicuously layered, but are softer than more intensely cooked rocks; they split and crumble more easily than the higher-grade metamorphic rocks found over most of central New England.

ဖော

BESIDES BEING FIREPROOF, DURABLE, AND SLABBY, NEW England's metamorphic fieldstones are usually conveniently shaped for stonework. Most often they have straight sides, sharp angles, well-defined corners, and are large enough to build with, yet small enough to manage easily by hand. Glaciers or ice sheets are popularly believed to be responsible for giving fieldstones these desirable attributes. This was certainly true for those stones with obvious crushing marks and snapped edges. But the fundamental process responsible for creating the convenient-size stones was the mechanical strain—expansion, contraction, shearing—imposed during the stone's vertical journey from mountain root to the Earth's surface, a distance of at least five miles straight up. By the time the glaciers arrived to pluck them up and scatter them about, most of the stones had already been broken in place, or they were preconditioned to break along closely spaced "lines of weakness" when roughly handled by the ice.

New England bedrock rose upward and ruptured into billions of straight-edged fragments as a consequence of "exhumation," a geological process caused by long-term erosion. The Acadian Mountains, which may have once been the tallest on Earth, are no longer there. In their place are the New England Plateau and the northern part of the Appalachian Mountains, tiny remnants of the range that once was there. They stand above the surrounding terrain because their rocks are harder and the crust is thicker beneath them.

When any mountain range is first eroded, miles of rock must be stripped away. As this weight is removed, the mountain roots rise upward to compensate for the loss of their "aboveground" counterparts, allowing rocks originally formed at great depths to rise upward through the crust. Exhumation also resembles the process in which the keel of a ship rises upward as its ballast or cargo is unloaded.

As New England's underground rocks were brought to the surface via exhumation, they expanded slightly in response to the drastically lower pressure, creating ubiquitous, three-dimensional stresses throughout the entire volume of rock. Stresses also occurred when the rock contracted due to cooler temperatures near the Earth's surface, and when the motion of tectonic plates caused horizontally directed pushes, pulls, and shearing movements.

At great depths rock fractures cannot exist because the rock is squeezed too tightly together by the overlying weight and is warm and malleable. Therefore, instead of breaking under tectonic stresses, they stretch and bend. Any fractures that do form are quickly healed by "creep," a solid-state flow in which the rocks behave plastically. But at a critical depth of several miles or so, rocks become less plastic and begin to break along incipient fractures. At higher levels, perhaps at a depth of a half mile or so, the rock is cold enough and the pressure is low enough that the incipient fractures can widen and intersect into visible openings, through which underground water flows. This breaking-up process increases exponentially in intensity the closer the rocks come to the Earth's surface. Rock breakage is also accentuated by earthquake shaking, by water pressure, and by fluctuations in the weight of thick ice sheets growing and receding on land.

Something analogous to rock fracturing takes place on glaciers today. Near the surface, where confining stress is low, the ice behaves as a brittle solid, breaking into a regular pattern of crevasses. Deep within the glacier, there are no crevasses because ice creeps instead of breaks. The same concept can be applied to the rocks of New England, which were pliable at depth, but which became hard as they rose near the surface. Angular fieldstones are analogous to shards of broken glacier ice that never melted: Rounded boulders are like shards that managed to melt at the corners.

ပာ

THE STRAIGHT-EDGE FRACTURES THAT CREATE ROCK SLABS are called joints. The simplest type of jointing is the hexagonal pattern of fractures that developed on the surface of a cooling lava flow where no other stresses were present to interfere or make the fracture pattern more complex. Granite can also fracture in highly regular shapes because it, too, cooled from a melt, although deep underground.

Most of New England's rocks, however, have a more complicated fracture pattern because there are multiple sets of fractures, each created in a separate tectonic regime after the rock first became rigid enough to break. The dominant set of joints is usually parallel to foliation and produces slabs of varying thicknesses. The second set of joints is often at right angles to foliation; this gives rise to vertical edges on slab-shaped stones. The third set of

A ledge outcrop showing intersecting joints.

joints usually cuts what would otherwise have been a book-shaped slab into a parallelogram-shaped one; acute and obtuse angles occur at adjacent corners. This last set is commonly produced by tectonic compression or extension. Such stones are easier to handle because the points of the stones (the acute angles of the parallelograms) provide excellent handholds.

Where the rocks were poorly layered during metamorphism, or where tectonic stresses were minimal, the pattern of jointing can be quite simple, giving rise to stones that are shaped like boxes or bricks. Rarest of all are prisms, which form only when large, homogeneous masses of magma cool in an environment free from tectonic twisting and stretching.

Regardless of shape, New England's near-surface bedrock is actually a tightly nested set of blocks and individual fragments bounded by joints. The glacier didn't break much rock from solid ledges because that kind of rock is much stronger than ice. But it did pluck up billions of blocks that broke during the exhumation process and were ready to be lifted away.

∾

BEGINNING ABOUT 50 MILLION YEARS AGO, SHORTLY AFTER the extinction of the dinosaurs, Earth began a long-term cooling trend. By 30 million years ago, some Antarctic ice was present. By 7 million years ago, large, permanent ice sheets had developed near both poles, inaugurating a prolonged period of glaciation matched only several times before in Earth history. In the process, the oceans became smaller, colder, and more compartmentalized. As sea level fell, more of the continents were exposed and they became colder. Low-latitude forests gave way to grassland, steppe, and savannah vegetation. Mammals, including early humans in Africa, were evolving.

Meanwhile, New England remained covered by lush, temperate forests, in which roamed exotic species related to deer, horses, pigs, camels, rhinoceroses, and other forms, now extinct. Its soils at this time were thick, clay-rich, and reddish brown in color, with hardly a surface stone. Would-be stones decomposed chemically along the joints before they reached the surface.

The onset of dramatic ice ages took place late in the Cenozoic period, during the last several million years, an epoch called the Pleistocene. During the Pleistocene, large ice sheets repeatedly developed near sixty degrees latitude, grew to enormous sizes, then oozed outward in all directions to inundate much of northern Europe, the northern United States, and much of the Siberian Plain.[2]

Largest of them all—four thousand miles in diameter and two miles thick at its center—was the Laurentide Ice Sheet, which expanded and contracted from central Canada in spasms of growth and decay. Never was it more enormous than when it covered New England between about fifteen thousand and thirty thousand years ago. There is evidence of at least three earlier Pleistocene glaciations in the region, although seven or more may have taken place. (The term "the Ice Age" is generally used to describe all of the advances and retreats within the past several million years.)

Curiously, the Laurentide Ice Sheet still exists today, surviving as a sluggish remnant called the Barnes Ice Cap, on Baffin Island, in the northeastern Canadian Arctic. Basal layers of its ice date back more than one hundred thousand years, indicating that this glacier "fossil" was once part of the larger, continent-size complex that covered New England, and which persisted over much of east-central Canada until six to eight thousand years ago, long after a well-documented human presence in the region. Layers of ice in the Barnes Ice Cap are the same age as layers deep beneath the center of the Greenland Ice Cap today.

As a result of ice sheets coming and going, the New England landscape was transformed from the chalky, clay-rich soil that had covered the land for tens of millions of

**Northern Hemisphere showing the Laurentide Ice Sheet
at maximum extent, 21,000 years ago.**

years to the fresher, rockier, sandier, more rugged landscape upon which the Puritans later would flourish.

Between each glaciation was a much longer period of
relative warmth called an interglaciation, when New
England was variously covered with forests, ponds, marshy
grasslands, and bogs.

Each glaciation began as a cooling trend, inaugurated
by changes in the Earth's orbit around the sun. These
changes involved times when the Earth's tilt became
greater, when its orbit became more elliptical, or when it
wobbled away from the sun during midsummer. These or-
bital changes, which were felt most strongly near sixty degrees latitude, combined to make summer temperatures
slightly warmer or slightly cooler than before. Patches of

snow that otherwise would have melted were instead transformed into granular masses of icy snow that managed to survive a subarctic summer somewhere in what is now Labrador and northern Quebec. After several such cool summers in a row (perhaps only three to four), formerly isolated snow patches coalesced into permanent snowfields that gradually became more compact, thicker, and broader every year.

At this point, growth of the ice sheet was inevitable because the process of snowfield growth was self-reinforcing. The bigger the snowfield, the cooler the local climate and the less snow melted, making the snowfield even larger. Within a few thousand years, such snowfields had merged into local ice caps the size of counties. These caps flowed toward each other, merging into ice sheets the size of states, which eventually merged into a single mass of ice stretching from Greenland to New England to Montana to the Yukon Territory. This was the largest transient ice sheet on Earth, dwarfing its only competitor, the Scandinavian Ice Sheet, which covered much of northern Europe, and which merged with ice on the British Isles.

Ice sheets don't just occupy the land. They are much more dynamic than overgrown ice cubes. Fundamentally, each ice sheet is a very weak solid that is unable to hold itself together, being brittle on the outside but soft in the middle where the pressure is greater. Each spreads outward under the influence of gravity, collapsing the way a ball of Silly Putty flattens if left on a table long enough. Ice sheets move in several ways, and may even leave the underlying landscape largely untouched. Usually they slide and scrape at a rate determined by the abundance of basal meltwater, which tends to float the glacier off its bed, and by the roughness of the underlying topography, which tends to retard forward motion. Sometimes they glide above a slurry of mud that is being churned and sheared until it behaves like a lubricated paste. Some parts of the ice sheet move at a rate of miles per year; others hardly move at all.

From its center just south of Hudson Bay, the Laurentide Ice Sheet flowed outward in all directions: east toward Labrador, north toward the Arctic Ocean, west toward the Rocky Mountains, southwest down the Great Lakes, and southeast toward New England. Even the Appalachian Mountains couldn't stop the Laurentide invasion. After flowing across the St. Lawrence River, it kept going until it reached the outer edge of the Atlantic coastal plain at Nantucket, Massachusetts. It did little damage to the tops of the mountains because it was probably frozen to the summits at that altitude. In the lowlands, however, it produced great change.

The ice sheet stopped growing in mass when the amount of ice melting along its southern fringe became equal to the amount moving in from the north. This caused the ice margin to stabilize in nearly the same position for thousands of years, oscillating back and forth slightly, never quite finding equilibrium. But even as the outer margin of the ice sheet stabilized, the ice within it kept flowing southward, scraping over the land with a velocity of inches per day, which is hundreds of times faster than that of continental drift. A good analogy to the way the Laurentide Ice Sheet ground away New England landscape is what happens when a belt sander is run while being held in the same place. Its belt is forever moving forward, shaping the wood block beneath it, creating gouges when the paper is coarse, and polishing it when it is fine.

To the east, the terminal position of the Laurentide Ice Sheet lay in the Gulf of Maine. Just east of Nantucket, however, the ice margin stood on dry land. The glacier margin continued west to Martha's Vineyard, Block Island, Fishers Island, and Long Island, then westward toward the Appalachians in Pennsylvania and the Great Lakes states.

These islands along the southern New England shoreline were physically thrust upward by the intermittent release of pressure created when the south-flowing glacier butted up against the north-facing edge of the Atlantic Coastal Plain. This discontinuous ridge of islands, now a sandy archipelago, marked the dry-land terminal "moraine" of the Laurentide Ice Sheet, its outermost glacially produced ridge.

Most of the sand at the core of these islands is crushed bedrock that washed southward from Canada, the Appalachian Highlands, the New England Plateau, and the coastal plain in dark, subglacial tunnels that formed a vast sub-Laurentide drainage system. Hundreds of cavelike portals once dotted the ice margin. From each gushed a noisy river carrying with it a heavy load of sand and silt.

As they flowed onward toward the distant sea, these streams dropped their copious load of sand, forming broad fans that coalesced in a downstream direction, the most conspicuous of which are the flat sand plains of Long Island and Cape Cod. Each of these fans was covered by thousands of dry, flat-topped bars, around which the channels were braided. Water would flow within them—often torrentially—only during the summer when precipitation fell as rain, instead of snow, and when the days were warm enough to melt sufficient ice. During the peak of the melt season or during outburst floods, the entire fan surfaces were underwater.

It is this sand—crushed from the land, washed in tunnels, and dumped at the ice margin—that washes back and forth on New England beaches today. Atlantic waves merely helped themselves to this seemingly endless supply of glacier-crushed sand, as sea level rose against the continental shelf during the last fifteen thousand years.

ᛒ

NOT ALL OF THE CRUSHED-UP LANDSCAPE ESCAPED TO THE southern moraine belt or to the sea. Much of it was retained inside the ice margin where it was smeared to the land as a thick paste of cold, stony mud, especially on the New England Plateau, where the rough land surface caught much of the sediment in transport. This sediment paste would eventually produce soils that were almost magical in their ability to absorb heavy rainfalls without violent runoff, yet could retain subsurface water during the driest days of late summer, keeping pastures green and cattle satisfied. These soils were perfect for growing hay and planting apple orchards.

During agricultural settlement, soils developed upon this glacial paste were considered stronger than sandy lowland soils, meaning that they would remain fertile much longer. The Reverend Timothy Dwight, the widely traveled president of Yale College during the Federalist period, bragged about soils developed on this otherwise cementlike material:

The Reverend Timothy Dwight

The hills of this country, and of New England at large, are perfectly suited to the production of grass. They are moist to their summits. Water is everywhere found on them at a less depth than in the valleys or on the plains. I attribute the peculiar moisture of these grounds to the stratum lying immediately under the soil, which throughout a great part of this country is what is here called the hardpan.[3]

At the other end of New England, near Bowdoin College in Maine, Samuel Deane, a respected late-eighteenth-century agricultural adviser, also saw hardpan as "a great benefit to the soil. For as no manures can easily penetrate it." By manure he meant any liquid nutrient.

What Dwight and Deane called hardpan is lodgment till—a dense, compacted, fine-grained stratum up to two hundred feet thick that was deposited on the land as the glacier slid by. The term "till" is of Scottish origin, referring to "a kind of coarse and obdurate land" because it is both hard and stony.[4] Indeed, there is plenty of lodgment till in the central and northern British Isles, something else they have in common with New England.

Lodgment till was a gift to the pioneers, with or without the stones. It provided a physical barrier that blocked the seepage into the earth of rainfall and snowmelt. This kept the soils moist, gave rise to perennial springs, and trapped the water in small ponds needed to water livestock. Agricultural soils developed on lodgment till were highly fertile because they were composed of microscopic pieces of glacially pulverized minerals that provided an enormous surface area for biological reactions in the soil, especially those that feed nutrients to plant roots. Lodgment till also produced a terrain of smoothly rolling hills that were usually steep enough to let the water drain away, yet gentle enough to prevent surface gullying. Rock-hard beneath the surface, lodgment till was strong enough to support the largest barns. Finally, the gently rolling till-covered landscapes allowed easy movement of humans and their creatures because there was little need to build bridges or avoid rock crags.

Lodgment till is almost single-handedly responsible for rural New England's bucolic image—gracefully curved hillside pastures framed by stone walls. Unlike the sandier soils of coastal bays and river bottoms, lodgment till holds many stones. But early farmers quickly learned to take the bad with the good, the stones with the otherwise moist, fertile, solid, smooth, almost perfect soil. So sought after were soils on patches of lodgment till that farmers went looking for stone as a clue to soil quality. In a settlement pattern that would reverse the siting practices of eighteenth-century villages, many eighteenth-century interior towns were located not in river valleys or coastal lowlands, but in the highest places where the lodgment till was thickest and most extensive.

 споя

LODGMENT TILL WAS CREATED WHEN COUNTLESS BLOCKS OF slate, schist, granite, and gneiss were plucked from ledges by moving ice, then forced downward to the bedrock under grinding, wet conditions. Most of these slabs didn't survive the trip because there was a heavy traffic of stones caught in the shear zone between the perpetually moving ice and the stationary hard-rock bed. As they moved southward, the stones battered each other and pressed against the bed until they were ruptured, crushed, ground, rubbed, and reduced to a wet, stony mud, a mixture that was one part water, one part pulverized rock, and one part residual stone. This stone "pudding" became stiffer as the glacier slowed down; it stiffened more as the water within the mud was squeezed away, and even more as the weight of the ice compacted it. The final result was a dense, almost cementlike substratum of the lodgment till. Although coarse and obdurate, it was the otherwise luxurious raw material on which New England's pastoral economy would be based.

Most gardeners have experienced till, especially when digging postholes for a garden. In New England, it is usually easy to shovel the first foot or so because the topsoil is loose, "fluffed" by roots and underground animal activity. The next foot is difficult because the stones, although loose within the soil, are hard to work around. But to shovel much deeper than two feet is nearly impossible, for that is where shovel strikes lodgment till. It's no wonder the colonists called it hardpan.

Stones are widely distributed within the till rather than concentrated only near ledges. The bedrock beneath the ice sheet had been a bumpy place, so stones carried along by the ice were randomly pushed left and right, ensuring the spread of stones over the whole landscape. Every farmer would get his share.

Lodgment-till landscapes are generally smooth. The crushed-up debris, moving like stiff cement at subglacial pressures, would plug up the holes and round off the corners of jagged rock surfaces like plaster being carried into a nail hole by a putty knife or trowel. Once deposited, the material was soft enough so that it could be shaped and streamlined by the ice moving above it. Often, the streamlining of till by moving ice formed long hills called drumlins. The shapes of drumlins resemble hard-boiled eggs cut lengthwise and placed upside down on a platter. Thousands of drumlins grace some parts of the Welsh countryside, where *druim* means "rounded hill" in Gaelic. They also occur widely in New England, upstate New York, and the Great Lakes states. America's most famous drumlin is Bunker Hill, near Boston. Sometimes the flanks of drumlins are furrowed deeply, as if carved by a plowshare. This can happen when a large block of rock gouges out the softer till below. Such gouges, and the drumlins they cut, are markers identifying lodgment-till landscapes.

Above the lodgment till in most places is a thinner, looser layer of stones and sand called ablation till.[5] As the ice sheet thinned and pulled back during its withdrawal, its outer fringe—a zone about a mile wide and more than a hundred feet thick—stopped moving forward before the ice could completely disappear. It became a dirty, stone-laden band of stagnant ice, no longer capable of moving forward. As the ice melted downward, any material within it became concentrated at the surface. Quite often a somewhat uniform layer of stony ablation till would slide into a pit on the stagnant glacier surface, concentrating it even further. Such "pockets" of stone could drive a farmer crazy, because they have no obvious explanation.

Stones from the ablation-till layer formed the bulk of most stone walls because they were abundant, large, angular, and easy to carry. In contrast, stones from lodgment till are often smaller, chunkier, and more rounded because they were beaten up during transport at the base of the ice. The most prominent stones from the ablation-till layer, however, were "glacial erratics," too big to move. The largest of these boulders in New England are the size of public buildings, although most are the size of automobiles. Plymouth Rock, the landmark boulder on the western side of Cape Cod Bay that allegedly marks the landing site of the Pilgrims, is a glacial erratic; it is now protected as a national shrine and tourist attraction. An erratic escaped being broken up if the ice sheet carried it just a short distance, or if the boulder was lifted high within the ice, above where rocks were being converted into lodgment till. Erratics are a study in power and grace—they are enormous, yet were set down upon the land gently as the last bit of ice melted away. A few of them rolled into odd positions before coming to rest, giving the illusion that they were placed there by prehistoric visitors or natives.

ဟၺ

The author's daughter standing next to an erratic rock.

NOT ALL OF INLAND NEW ENGLAND IS STONY. IN CONTRAST, there are thousands of flat, sandy, generally low areas without a stone in sight for a mile in any direction. In such places, the stones are hidden, deeply buried by the grit of ground-up rocks that washed away from the ice margin. One of the causes of sediment being focused in basins involves the weight of the Laurentide Ice Sheet. It was so heavy that it dimpled the Earth's crust downward into the soft upper mantle, creating a huge bowl-shaped depression, although Hudson's Bay is the only large surviving remnant of its bowl. Each year, this bay becomes a little smaller as the land beneath it rises, uplift that began when the ice above it began to melt twenty thousand years ago.

New England, especially to the north where the ice was thicker, lay near the edge of this ice-loaded bowl. The buildup of ice was slow enough for the crust and mantle to respond; the land surface was pushed downward to well below sea level. As the ice disappeared, however, it melted faster than the crust could respond, allowing the sea to flood every low spot. The St. Lawrence Lowland, near Montreal, Lake Champlain, straddling the border of Vermont with New York, and the large rivers of south-central Maine were all once arms of the sea. Sediments deposited in these once-salty bodies of water contain the bones of Ice Age whales and other salt-loving creatures.

The great depression of the crust also caused rivers to flow more sluggishly to the sea when the glaciers were pulling back. Where such rivers flowed across lowlands, especially old rift basins, the valleys were easily flooded by ribbon-shaped glacial lakes. Long Island Sound was once a freshwater lake—icy cold and battleship gray in color—nearly the size of Lake Ontario. Block Island Sound, in Rhode Island, and Buzzards Bay and Cap Cod, in Massachusetts, were also freshwater lakes, each dammed in by their respective segments of the terminal moraine.

Streams draining southward into these ribbon- and moat-shaped lakes carried a staggering load of sand and silt when the ice receded between eleven and eighteen thousand years ago. Quite often, the smaller lakes were overwhelmed with sediment, which built up as sandy deltas and braided floodplains. The largest lakes, however, drained before they were completely filled, leaving extensive, extremely flat, clay-rich plains, like those of the Connecticut River Valley and Hudson Valley. The same is true of Long Island Sound. Its old lake bed was once exposed to the wind and gashed by gullies before being flooded by the rising sea. Beneath the surface lies nearly four hundred feet of lake mud.

The smaller, stone-free coastal lowlands north of

Boston, especially along the coast of central Maine, have a different origin. No large lakes existed there. Instead, the heavy load of glacial sediment was deposited directly into the sea and its tidewater estuaries before the Earth's crust could flex back upward to its original position. In the process, the muddy, brackish estuaries were physically lifted above the sea, forming broad terraces now more than 150 feet above sea level.

∾

IN MOST OF NEW ENGLAND—VIRTUALLY THE ENTIRE SUR-FACE of the interior plateau—settlers found a landscape underlain by lodgment till and draped by ablation till. Next in abundance, they encountered the glacial lake-bottom alluvial landscape dominated by sand and silt. There are, however, patches of other landscape types, none of which provided the agricultural opportunities of the above.

With respect to agriculture, the worst terrain in New England, that of jumbled, dry ledges, was usually washed "bare to the bone" by torrents of subglacial meltwater. Most such places, being even too rough for pasture, were used as farm wood lots, where pine was culled for timber, chestnut for fence rails, hemlock for bark, sugar maples for sap, and much of what remained for firewood, avoiding resinous soft woods and elm. A good-size farmhouse in New England burned up to thirty-five cords of wood per year. So even this land had significant value.

Second worst were the local patches of sand dunes, which formed in the sandy lowlands where winds gusted along the edge of the ice sheets above unvegetated terrain. On the eastern side of the Connecticut River Valley, near the boundary between Connecticut and Massachusetts, lies the former bottomland of glacial Lake Hitchcock, which gave rise to the largest sand dunes in New England, nearly half a mile long and barn size in cross section. These inland sandlots were later stabilized with drought-loving pine and oak scrub forests. Similar, but less well-defined, tracts of shifting late-Pleistocene dunes also covered much of Cape Cod, Long Island, and southeastern Maine. More locally, dunes formed on nearly every abandoned lake bed, especially on their eastern shores, because the prevailing winds during the dry season were westerly.

English settlers were initially attracted to these sandy soils because they could be easily cleared by burning, and because the stumps, being rooted in sand, were easy to remove. The Native Americans had known this as well. Unfortunately, these wind-blown soils turned out to be among the worst for agricultural purposes, especially for pasture, because they were excessively dry when located above the water table, and constantly wet when below it. Many acres of drifting dunes in colonial New England— the sand desert midway up Maine's eastern shore, the dunes of Provincetown, at the tip of Cape Cod, and the sand plains of New Haven—are the overgrazed remnants of these Ice Age deserts. They persist not because there is too little rain, but because the rain that does fall infiltrates too fast for its moisture to be retained. These were the damaged soils that caught the attention of New England's first agricultural reformers like Jared Eliot, who noted problems even before the American Revolution.

Bad soils, at least from the point of view of agriculture, also occurred on the dry, boulder-studded valley-bottom landscapes where torrents of glacial meltwater deposited ridges, terraces, and patches of coarse gravel and sand, usually in small stream valleys. Such patches are called eskers if deposited in subglacial tunnels, and kame terraces if deposited against the edges of down-wasting ice. Downstream from the zone of coarse gravel and sand, however, most small New England valleys were once occupied by braided sandy streams called valley trains that often left sediment too well drained and too deficient in nutrients for good pasture. Missing from these soils was the mineral silt that makes lodgment till so fertile. It had been washed away to the glacial lakes at lower elevations.

ဟဃ

EVENTUALLY, ALL OF NEW ENGLAND'S GLACIAL LANDFORMS were exposed to the sun, wind, and rain. In the till-covered uplands, exposure to the elements concentrated the surface stone through erosion. This was especially true during the earliest postglacial millennia when the climate was windy and moist, the winters long, and the ground froze deeply and thawed quite late. Without vegetation to protect the soil and to make it porous, and with the ground being frozen much of the year, rainfall and snowmelt did not infiltrate effectively. Instead, even small rainstorms caused considerable runoff, which washed over the surface, winnowing sand and silt from the till and leaving the stones in place, sometimes armoring the surface with a pavement of stone. Stone was also being heaved upward by frost in the soil, a process that preferentially lifts larger stones to the surface. With erosion concentrating soils from the top down, and with frost heave bringing stones up from below, the uplands hillsides quickly became stony and barren, a cold, rocky desert.

Inevitably, the austere hostility of the last Ice Age

would give way to interglacial conditions, a time of life rather than of ice. The "moonscape" left by the withdrawal of ice from New England would—for the seventh or eighth time—be transformed back into a lush, forested ecosystem. Gray, rocky till would give way to a carpet of green. The stones would give way to soil. But this interglacial landscape would be different from all that had come before it because of the arrival of human beings. Soon after the ice retreated, Paleo-Indian peoples migrated into what is now the northeastern United States. They hunted mammoths and other Ice Age beasts, leaving fossils of stone knives and butchered animal remains. Twelve thousand years later, people from the other side of the ocean arrived, bringing with them the tools of change: axes, plows, oxen, shovels, and chains. These English farmers would be agents of environmental change whose power was exceeded only by that of the ice.

3

~

Burying the Stone

S THE ICE SHEET WITHDREW TO THE NORTH, IT LEFT in its wake a lifeless, rocky, rubbly, windswept landscape. Nothing except a few bacteria had been able to grow beneath the glacier. Boulders and rock fragments lay everywhere, especially on the uplands. Soil was absent; the land had been stripped down to its essence. The landscape was all grays and browns, except for countless ponds and lakes, which turned blue under sunny skies as the silt within them settled to the bottom.

Fifteen thousand years later, most of the ponds had been filled and turned into marshes and swamps. Only the deepest, cleanest, largest ponds and lakes remained. A thick, black, luxurious organic soil had developed over nearly everything else, burying most of the glacially scattered stones in the uplands, and mulching the sandy soils of the alluvial and coastal lowlands. These soils, when prepared for seed or mowed for hay, would become the most important and indispensable natural resource in early America.

~

SOIL IS VIRGIN BEFORE IT IS "TAKEN" BY THE PLOW. THE plow's iron tip penetrates the turf, then the leading edge of the plow slices small roots and cleaves the soil. Next the plowshare, the gracefully curved part of the tool, forces the original layers to turn over like a breaking wave, turning the soil upside down, inverting its vividly colorful layers. The top layer, a brown rug of fibrous roots, becomes the bottom. Virgin humus (decayed plant material) is the consistency of black butter. It is followed by layers of ashen-gray, reddish-brown, and yellow soil. All rise up and fall into the adjacent furrow.

After the plow comes the harrow, whose spiky teeth break the clods apart, then rake them smooth. The manure wagon spreads its aromatic blessing and the soil is raked once again. No longer virgin, this "plow zone" has the bland, fertile color familiar to every gardener. It is ready for seed.

Rich soil develops automatically whenever three ingredients come together: plant life, water, and the remains of broken-up rocks—whether crushed stone, gravel, sand, silt, or clay. Soil has the power to regenerate itself, even from the rubble left by ice sheets, or the cobble of trodden pastures. Soil requires life, but gives life back in full return. Ralph Waldo Emerson, chief architect of Transcendentalism, the first serious break with the Congregational doctrine brought to America by the Pilgrims, understood this:

> *From air the creeping centuries drew*
> *The matted thicket low and wide,*
> *This must the leaves of ages strew*
> *The granite slab to clothe and hide,*
> *Ere wheat can wave its golden pride.*[1]

Emerson's "air" refers to the gases of nitrogen, oxygen, and carbon dioxide, which are converted into plant tissue—

sugars, lipids, carbohydrates—by photosynthesis. His "matted thicket" is the dense concentration of roots in the humus that vigorously attacks and recycles the nutrients from strewn leaves. The Earth's crust and its mineral soil, here alluded to as a "granite slab," becomes "hidden" over time by the by-product of biology, the soil.

The contemporary view is that colonial agricultural soils were stony and difficult to work. However, Peter Kalm, from the University of Abo in Sweden, a professional botanist who toured New England during the colonial period, made a glowing assessment of its forest soils: "Thus the upper fertile soil increased considerably, for centuries; and the Europeans coming to America found a rich, fine soil before them, lying loose between the trees as the best bed in a garden. They had nothing to do but to cut down the wood, put it up in heaps, and to clear the dead leaves away." Timothy Dwight agreed, noting that the rich agricultural soils of the New England Plateau came from "grounds long forested."[2]

Indeed, the story of New England's soils is connected to its forest history, one that began when the first hardy plants migrated northward to colonize the rubble left in the wake of the retreating ice.[3] Within a few millennia, New England would be transformed from a jagged, austere land of rocky shadows into a smooth, treeless, green landscape called tundra. This ground-hugging plant community—dominated by sedge, grass, willow, dwarf birch, and heather—took shelter beneath the boulders, then spread outward in blotches until it formed a continuous carpet of lowland tundra, broken only by protruding stones and ledges.

Tundra is white in the winter when covered with snow, the golden-brown color of hay in autumn and early spring, and the vivid green color of fast-growing grass during its brief but luxurious growing season, between mid-May and mid-August. Lowland tundra, an ecosystem so abundant in the barren lands of northern Canada, has long since disappeared from New England, except for tiny windswept patches on Maine's "down-east" coast. Alpine tundra still exists on northern Appalachian summits, including Mount Washington, the highest peak in the eastern United States. Only above tree line is the terrain cold and windy enough for tundra to survive.

The gradual spread of lowland tundra helped trap the dust blowing in from the melting ice margin to the north and the west, where the lobes of the ice sheet lingered longer. The ice-margin dust supply was maintained long after local retreat because the continent-size pile of ice generated its own south-draining wind regime. Dust was generated in several ways: from shifting dunes that were migrating across old glacial-lake shorelines; from the floodplains of braided meltwater streams, where the annual snowmelt floods and dramatic outburst floods kept the river bottoms unvegetated; and from the till surface itself, especially where frost was churning muddy spots, or where the earliest invading insects and their predators—small mammals like lemmings and voles—were burrowing.

The spread of tundra and the dust-gathering process was self-perpetuating. The more vegetation, the more dust trapped; the more dust trapped, the more vegetation, and so on. Trapped dust was being claimed for the future soil. As the dust thickened with time, the barren expanses of gray till were first dotted, then blotched by velvet-green tundra, beneath which the stones, especially slabby ones lying flat on the surface, were being thinly covered by the first soils.

By fourteen thousand years ago, forests began to invade southern New England, beginning with patches of boreal coniferous species. Slowly, the tundra landscape was transformed into parkland where clumps of trees grew among an otherwise continuous blanket of grass and sedge. Mastodons browsed at the woodland edge. Caribou grazed in the open. Paleo-Indian hunters stalked both kinds of creatures, slaughtering them with stone-tipped spears, then roasting the meat on open fires circled by stones. Other predators migrated northward as well, notably wolves, bears, and even mountain lions, which the colonists later would call panthers.

Then the climate warmed abruptly about eleven thousand years go. The parkland receded as forests began to dominate the landscape and conifers encroached on the last remaining patches of sedge and grass. By ten thousand years ago, summer conditions were as warm as those of colonial times. Forest species, previously limited by the cold temperatures, proliferated rapidly northward, replacing those that were better adapted to the cooler, moister conditions of early postglacial time.

The modern forests of New England are in transition between the continuous hardwood, broadleaf forests of the Appalachians to the south, and the trackless conifer forests to the north, in Canada.[4] In the southern part of the transition zone, the trees are largely deciduous (oak, hickory, chestnut, ironwood, elm, beech). To the north, the forests become progressively more coniferous (birch, pine, fir, spruce). Pine occupies dry sites throughout the region; red maple and alder flourish in the swamps. This transitional forest spans a range of latitudes from as far south as Long Island, New York, to the northern part of Maine, and an even broader range of local conditions— south versus north slopes, wet versus dry, rocky versus loamy. New England forests are noted less for their species richness than for their geographic diversity.

Even after the deciduous canopy was complete, about eight thousand years ago, the composition of the species within it kept changing, owing to historic processes such as the continuing in-migration of plant and animal species. Trees whose seeds dispersed northward more slowly lagged behind those that migrated rapidly. When the seedlings of late arrivals sprouted, they competed with the already established pioneering trees. In-migrating birds and small mammals also changed the patterns of seed dispersal. Insect, fungal, viral, and otherwise unspecified pathogens caused some species to die, leaving room for others to flourish. Hurricanes and ice storms became quite selective in terms of which type of tree they blew down most frequently. Patches of anomalous vegetation expanded, contracted, and jumped about on the landscape. Deer exploded onto the scene when one of their principal food staples, acorns, arrived with the oak forest. Their predators included the Archaic Indians, a hunting and fishing culture thousands of years ago. Throughout it all, the forest was always changing. The soil was always thickening. The dry stone habitat was diminishing.

ဖဖ

MANY ANTIQUARIANS AND AMATEUR ARCHAEOLOGISTS SWEAR that some New England stone ruins were built thousands of years ago by Vikings, Celts, Druids, or Native Americans prior to European contact. Busloads of tourists each year go to Gungywamp, Connecticut, to examine odd circles of stone in the swamp. Wiccan groups meet there as well, drawn to the mysterious woodland scene for their midnight events. At the other end of New England, thousands of tourists visit what is called America's Stonehenge in North Salem, New Hampshire, to see ceremonial "kivas," lintels in the middle of nowhere, and odd "standing" stones. Gungywamp and America's Stonehenge are not natural rock formations, although there remains some controversy over when they were built and by whom. Dating the stone itself is not yet possible in this situation, but the structures are younger than the glacial soils on which they sit and at least one hundred years old, because it took that long for the stones to be stained gray, covered with lichen, and for the surface to be roughed up by the elements.

Native Americans of the northeastern woodlands, prior to European contact, did move some stones around, but they did not have a stone-building tradition. They hauled a few rocks from their agricultural fields, used stone to make fire pits, buried their dead beneath rock piles, made soup with hot pebbles, and stacked a few stones, perhaps just to make a seat. But otherwise they left a negligible ecological footprint on the mineral soil. There are no monumental pyramids, pueblos, mounds, and extensive irrigated fields, which are widespread in the West and to a lesser extent in the Southeast. Nothing close to that "footprint on the land" is seen in the Northeast. Instead, Native Americans there scattered their arrowheads widely and left a few of their tools behind, especially at lowland village and mortuary sites. As a rule, prehistoric archaeological sites in the rolling hills of upland New

England are small and extremely rare. The most dramatic human impacts on the land from late prehistory were the occasional burnings of patches of dry forest.[5]

The limited use of stone by the Native Americans in the northeastern woodlands was due to their relatively small populations and their migratory lifestyle, moving from place to place seasonally. But fundamentally, the absence of stonework indicates that they had neither the desire nor the power to dig deeply in the densely rooted postglacial soils of the deciduous forest. Instead of being eroded—as was the case in so much of the Old World after the Neolithic agricultural revolution about ten thousand years ago—the upland forest soil of New England kept on forming and growing and thickening right up to the time when it was first cleared of trees and plowed by European immigrants. Essentially, the entire span of time between deglaciation and the arrival of the first Europeans was a quiet one in terms of landscape processes in the upland. The wind, rain, sun, and forest creatures were busy making soil, transforming the rubble of deglaciation into the lush, woody world that would one day be encountered by the colonists.

∽∾

THE LANDSCAPE HISTORIAN JOHN STILGOE, QUOTING OBSERVATIONS made by an unnamed Dutch visitor in 1656, uncovered the following technically precise early description of northeastern soils:

> *The surface of the land generally is composed of a black soil intermixed with clay, about a foot or a foot and a half deep, and in some places more, and some places less; below, the*

*stratum is white, reddish, and yellow clay,
which in some places is mixed with sand, and
in others with gravel and stones. [The soils]
are wonderfully fertile, which in short, is the
general quality of such land, and of most of
the places we have noticed.*[6]

Similar though less precise descriptions written during the seventeenth and eighteenth centuries are quite
common, even for sites in the uplands of New England.
Generally speaking, early observers viewed the soil as fertile, generally black, often multicolored, and up to two feet
thick above the stony or gravelly subsoil. Even the first

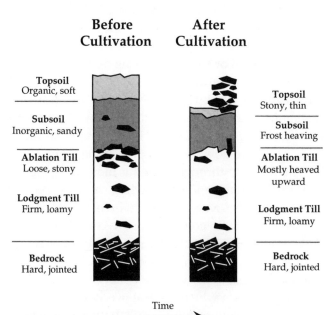

**Before
Cultivation**   **After
Cultivation**

Topsoil
Organic, soft

Topsoil
Stony, thin

Subsoil
Inorganic, sandy

Subsoil
Frost heaving

Ablation Till
Loose, stony

Ablation Till
Mostly heaved
upward

Lodgment Till
Firm, loamy

Lodgment Till
Firm, loamy

Bedrock
Hard, jointed

Bedrock
Hard, jointed

Time

Changes in soil layers before and after deforestation.

American dictionary definition of soil, by Samuel Deane (1790), was explicit in equating the word "soil" to only the upper, more finely textured horizons: "That part of the earth which lies upon the hard understratum, over which there is commonly a cover of rich mould, which forms the surface, unless destroyed by severe burning, or washed off by violent rains, or blown away by driving winds."[7]

The black topsoil is a mixture of humus and mineral matter, generally ranging from sand to clay in particle size. It lies immediately beneath the zone of dense rootlets, and is formed by the oxygenated, bacterial decomposition of litter, which recycles the organic nutrients—phosphorus, nitrogen, and carbon—back to tree roots during each growing season. The nutritive value of black topsoil was recognized as early as the seventeenth century by the scientist John Evelyn, who described it as "The most beneficial sort of mould or Earth, appearing on the surface, is the natural under-turf Earth."

Beneath the black topsoil are often three horizons of finer-grained materials (sand, silt, and clay), formed when rainwater, especially from drenching summer storms, was able to percolate downward to underlying aquifers, modifying the material through which it moved.[8] Immediately below the black topsoil is the "white" horizon, one so severely leached by New England's naturally acidic water that it is light gray in color, and relatively infertile. Next is a dark reddish-brown horizon, stained by the accumulation of iron oxides and organic acids washed down from above. Below that is the mineral material—called the parent material—from which the soil was derived. Its yellowish to brownish-yellow color is due to the staining by iron-bearing waters ("chalybeate" was the colonial term) that were leaching downward toward the water table.

The New England climate, and the life it generates, is punishing to the parent material, whether rock, till, gravel, sand, dust, or clay. Abundant spring rain leads to heavy, rapidly growing trees, whose large roots cling to ledges and help pry them apart. Roots also penetrate into the ablation- and lodgment-till layers, loosening them dramatically and causing them to expand. The warmth of summer activates microbes in the soil that, in the process of consuming organic matter, release corrosive by-products such as carbonic, fulvic, and humic acids. These caustic substances, in the presence of infiltrating water, transform silicate minerals of the till into rust and clay. Summer is also the time when the soil becomes alive with countless invertebrates, from crickets to mites, all of which break up the soil in some way. Autumn hurricanes uproot trees, which tear stones off ledges and sometimes lift them from deep within the till toward the surface, where they are attacked by the elements. In winter, the pressure of ice building up in cracks causes many stones to split into fragments, which then break into smaller fragments, and so on. Blocks of rock can even be ejected straight upward from ledges by the pressure of ice growing underground. The climate seems to be at war with the Earth's crust, with the soil as their battleground.

Water, the principal weapon in this conflict, was actually once part of the rock. All of Earth's water originally came from its primitive crust, having been boiled out of lava billions of years ago. Nearly all of this water has since gone back and forth, into and out of rock, many times, when water trapped in marine sediments was forced deep into the crust during the mountain-building process, then boiled off later as volcanic steam. Nearly all of the metamorphic rocks of New England would be full of water to-day had it not been squeezed and steamed out of Iapetos sediments when the Acadian mountains were being born. Once liberated back to the atmosphere as part of this slow hydrologic cycle, water is free to circulate in the familiar, and much faster, hydrologic cycle, going from rain to river to sea to vapor to clouds, then back to rain.[9]

ᴄᴂ

WATER, IN THE PROCESS OF MAKING SOIL, IS CHEMICALLY changed. All water seeping through soil and circulating near the Earth's surface, including urban tap water, carries with it the dissolved constituents of rocks that escaped from the soil. In terms of rock type, marble is dissolved most easily, followed by brownstone, slate, schist, and gneiss, then granite. Of the elements, sodium most easily leaches from the soil into the groundwater, followed by calcium, then potassium, and then magnesium. If not ad-sorbed onto fine soil particles or drawn into roots of plants, this dilute stone soup seeps down to the water table, where it flows slowly but surely from aquifers to streams, springs, wetlands, wells, and the sea. It is for this reason that the sea is salty.

After the alchemy of making soil, after all this soaking, leaching, washing, reacting, and draining, all that is left of the original parent material are coarse-grained resistant fragments the size of pebbles and stones; fine-grained re-sistant particles composed of stable mineral crystals such as quartz (silt and sand-size); a host of microscopic oxides and clay minerals; and dissolved ions. If the coarse-grained particles are resistant to further mechanical and chemical breakdown, they generally stay within the soil, whereas the dissolved ions, fine-grained clays, and the silts are easily flushed to the sea, along the way making rivers turbid. The fine-grained resistant particles can be washed to streams and rivers as sand, but more often they stay within the soil, where they are moved about by forest plants and animals.

When first produced from rock or released from the till, both the coarse-grained and the fine-grained resistant particles are mixed together within the soil. But as the soil develops, the coarse and fine particles become separated into a finer-grained upper part of the soil and a coarser-grained lower part—as a result of animal activity, plant processes, and stone decomposition.[10]

Charles Darwin was the first to scientifically describe how small creatures (in his case, earthworms) actually *create* topsoil, something he called "vegetable mould." This happens as a by-product of their primary daily activity: ingesting soil, passing it through their guts, then leaving "worm casts" that make the soil looser and more granular than before.

Worms don't actually create new mineral soil or organic matter. But by constantly stirring the soil, they inevitably concentrate finer-grained material nearer the surface. Everything too big for a worm to move will sink as part of the stirring process, partly because it is denser than the surrounding loosened soil. The primary reason, however, is that stones either remain where they are or move downward, whereas the finer-grained materials can move either up or down. The net effect is to sink coarse fragments.

Sandier soils, which are common throughout New England, especially when beneath conifers, are too acidic for significant earthworm activity. In these soils, ants are the most important agent in stirring soils. Several species of ants not only survive New England's harsh winter, but reproduce at astonishing rates. They are constantly busy within the soil, bringing fine-grained material to the surface and, in the process, sinking the stones. Building on Darwin's work, and focusing on ants, the nineteenth-century Harvard geology professor Nathaniel Shaler examined a four-acre field in Cambridge, Massachusetts. He estimated that common ants brought enough particles to the surface that, if spread out evenly, would cover the entire field at a rate of "a fifth of an inch" each year:

> *One of the most curious effects arising from the interference of the ants with the original conditions of the soil consists in the separation of the finer detritus from the coarse mineral elements of the detrital layer. I long ago had occasion to observe that in certain parts of New England, where the sandy soils had not for a long time been exposed to the plow ... certain fields were covered to the depth of some inches by a fine sand without pebbles larger than the head of a pin ... while deeper parts of the section ... were mainly composed of pebbles of various sizes with little finer material among them.*[11]

In the early 1960s, Walter Lyford, a soil scientist, extended Shaler's investigations in his study of Harvard Forest in Petersham, Massachusetts. There, he estimated that common ants could carry to the surface the equivalent of ten to eighteen inches of soil in a period of three to four thousand years. At this rate, two to four feet of fine-grained soils could have been produced in the last fifteen thousand years by ants alone.

Ants are not the only creatures to change the texture of the soil. Grubs, millipedes, insects, moles, shrews, mice, spiders, and many other burrowing animals assist in the process as well. Any small creature digging downward must lift (or push) fine-textured material upward, causing larger material to sink. Even horizontal burrows help sink stones because the animals digging them more often go below a stone than above it in order to protect the burrow from surface predators or exposure. When the tunnels collapse, as they must, stones above them will descend with the soil. Over thousands of animal lifetimes, and millions of tunnels, large stones eventually become concentrated at depth.

Similarly, the roots of plants affect the concentration of stones. Tree roots leave tubes within the soil after the roots die and decompose; stones can, and usually do, fall downward into these tubes; they cannot fall upward. And the stone need not fall all the way to the bottom of the tube for this process to be effective; a slight settling for each dead root multiplied by thousands of dead roots per millennium is sufficient to sink the stone.

Most of the processes causing the disintegration of stone—frost shattering, chemical weathering, and the prying action of roots—reach their maximum expression near the surface. Therefore, deeper stones last longer, so, over time, there are more of them.

The concentrating of stones in the subsoil by animal, plant, and weathering processes occurs ubiquitously and silently throughout the woodlands. Only rarely do we have

a chance to gauge its rate. The St. John's Bridge archaeological site in northwestern Vermont provides such an opportunity.[12] There, on a low terrace just above a curve in
the railroad, large limestone fragments, thrown up onto
the soil by dynamite explosions associated with a realign-
ment of the tracks in the 1850s, have already been sunk to
the base of the fine-grained topsoil. They lie a foot below
the modern surface, mixed into a stony horizon containing
Native American artifacts from the Archaic period. Biological stirring sank the stones in little more than a century.
Using a more general example, brick fragments often
found near the base of urban garden lots were sunk in
place by many of the same processes that made the gardens grow.

Conversely, stone can be raised by some processes.
(These are discussed in more detail in Chapter 5.) Frost
heave raises stone only when the raw soil is exposed to
the cold atmosphere; otherwise the snow (if present) and
organic matter (leaf litter, mulch, root zone, and organic-
rich topsoil) insulate the soil so effectively that it cannot
freeze below the surface. The natural uprooting of trees
also raises a few stones in their tipped-up mass of roots,
but these usually fall back into the hole from which they
were lifted. Debris flows, usually the combined product of
steep slopes and torrential rain, can carry stones downhill,
leaving them above a vegetated surface; but this process is
rare in the heavily forested slopes of the New England region. These processes, and many others, are locally intense
but are regionally far less significant than the slow biological forces that sink large stone fragments into the soil.[13]

By the time the European colonists arrived, the upland
soil had been developing and thickening for at least twelve

thousand years, producing a thick, mixed organic and mineral soil beneath old-growth forests that was "spongy underfoot." The pioneers, axes in hand, would find few stones visible on the surface. But beneath the seductive veneer of "vegetable mould," the stones lay in waiting. Many were encountered as the first postholes were dug for fences. Thousands more would soon rise up from the dark soil and be whitewashed by spring rains. There was simply no way for early settlers to determine accurately how many stones were hidden in the soil until they actually emerged. In this regard, guessing the stoniness of the subsoil was like playing the lottery.

ဖာ

IN THE LOWLANDS, WHERE GLACIAL GRAVEL, SAND, SILT, AND clay accumulated, there were no stones to sink and concentrate because they had already been deeply buried. On terraces well above the reach of the sea or river floods, soil formation was generally similar to that on the till-covered uplands. But in the true lowlands of broad floodplains, estuaries, and marshes, the continued burial of the stone wasn't due chiefly to biological processes, but to the steady rise of the sea.[14]

Global sea level has been rising since the onset of deglaciation, about twenty thousand years ago. Essentially, as glaciers melted off the land, the water from which they were made was returned to the sea. Because the volume of the world's ocean basins didn't change much, adding the water from continent-size ice sheets caused the upper surface of the sea—marked by high tide—to rise against the land. The pace of global sea-level rise picked up dramatically between eleven and fourteen thousand years ago, when glaciers throughout the world were rapidly melting and breaking up into icebergs. The rise of the sea was so fast at this time that coastal lowlands were quickly flooded; there wasn't enough time for sediment—normally pushed up by waves or brought down by rivers—to accumulate. Hence, the shoreline zone remained narrow and rough. Bays were deep, beaches narrow, deltas tiny, and marshes didn't exist.

Beginning about nine thousand years ago, however, the pace at which the sea encroached on the land slowed because there was less glacier ice left in the world to melt. With more time for the sea to shape the shoreline, intertidal zones became well established. Beaches widened. Coastal marshes began to form. Large deltas began to grow throughout the world, especially between seven and nine thousand years ago: the Euphrates in Iraq, the Nile in Egypt, the Ganges and the Indus in India, the Mackenzie in Canada's Yukon Territory, and the Yangtsze in China.

Beginning about three to four thousand years ago, the inundation of the New England shore slowed down to a fraction of an inch per year. For the first time in over ten thousand years, the pace of shoreline sedimentation was able to keep up with the rate of rise in sea level. The marshes widened dramatically, then grew slowly upward, producing thick peat soils. Cut into them were countless tidal inlets through which tidal currents could flow, and in which aquatic life could thrive. Narrow beaches grew broader, especially in protected bays where spits grew downwind from resistant coastal headlands. Blowing sand formed dunes that stabilized otherwise transient sandbars. Elsewhere, coastal bluffs retreated, leaving behind broad, stony intertidal zones full of edible marine life.

Farther upstream, rivers at the head of each estuary began to flow more sluggishly. They dropped their loads of silt and clay carried from countless tributaries and stream banks into their watersheds. Sediment deposition in channel bottoms caused the rivers to flood with greater frequency. Layer after layer of sediment accumulated on the channel banks, creating extensive floodplains—complete with meandering channels, broad river sandbars, and crescent-shaped freshwater marshes in abandoned channels.

Floodplain development was also taking place above the reach of the sea, especially in the largest river valleys. The load of ice was long gone. Rivers had already cut down through the glacial sediment basins as deeply as they could because they were bounded by bedrock ledges and concentrations of boulders. No longer able to deepen, river valleys widened instead, eroding material from their banks and carrying it downstream, where it was redeposited in the next broad bend of the river. Such broad, open lowlands along large rivers, called interval lands, were produced by the slow upward accretion of these alluvial soils.

For all except the last two or three centuries of the postglacial epoch, these alluvial and estuarine lowland soils, rather than their upland counterparts, guided human life in New England. During the Archaic period, Native Americans developed an economy based largely on estuarine resources: fish, shellfish, and other marsh creatures. During the subsequent Woodland period, which lasted until European contact, Indians planted crops—principally maize, squash, and beans—on the floodplains and low terraces near the coast and in upstream interval lands. Europeans, who first began to explore New England in the sixteenth century, restricted their searches to the coast and its broad tidewater rivers, especially the Connecticut and Hudson Rivers. Later, when the first colonies were settled, they, too, were restricted to these lowlands, in part because their cattle were dependent on natural meadows, areas kept clear of trees by seasonal flooding. This was especially important during the earliest phase of colonization, when most of the interior woodlands were not yet cleared for pasture.

Later settlers ventured above the level of annual flooding (but below the level of the highest annual floods, then called freshets) to find the very best tillage soils of New England—moist but not too wet, and periodically recharged with mineral nutrients. Abandoned river channels contained wet marshes and swamps that were exploited for their cedar and game animals, particularly venison. Cartloads of swamp soil (called muck) were hauled off as compost. Peat, another lowland organic soil, was burned as fuel, but only by the earliest Irish immigrants. Farming communities in the Connecticut River Lowland would eventually become the "breadbasket" of New England, owing to an almost perfect combination of flat topography, tidewater accessibility, freshwater, and very fertile soils.

It was the quality of these lowland alluvial soils that helped keep the majority of settlers away from the stony upland soils during much of the colonial period.

4

Taking the Forest

FIELDSTONE WALLS ARE CLOSELY ASSOCIATED WITH the colonial American landscape. Paintings from the era of the Revolutionary War show them in the background of rural life, or as battlements used by the colonial militia to protect them from British fire. Longfellow made the connection poetically in his chronicle of Paul Revere's ride, in which the minutemen of Lexington and Concord gave the redcoats "ball for ball from behind each and every farmyard wall." The association between stone walls and colonial times is indeed real, especially on the outskirts of ancient towns like Concord, the oldest inland town of the commonwealth, but it is greatly exaggerated. The truth is that thick stone walls were quite rare during the colonial era, especially in the first century and a half of settlement.

Early chronicles, including Captain John Smith's *Voyages* (1618), William Bradford's *History of Plymouth Plantation* (1620 to 1646), Francis Higginson's *New-England's Plantation* (1630), Thomas Morton's *New English Canaan* (1632), William Wood's *New England Prospect* (1634), John Winthrop's *Journal* (1630 to 1649), and John Josselyn's *Two Voyages to New England* (1674)

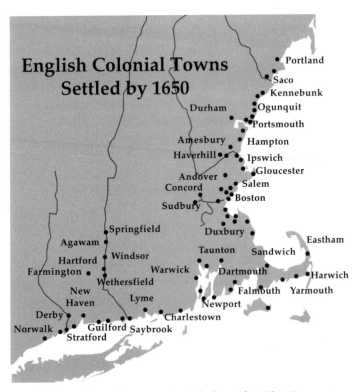

English Colonial Towns Settled by 1650

Portland
Saco
Kennebunk
Durham
Ogunquit
Portsmouth
Amesbury
Hampton
Haverhill
Ipswich
Andover
Gloucester
Concord
Salem
Sudbury
Boston
Springfield
Duxbury
Agawam
Eastham
Taunton
Sandwich
Hartford
Windsor
Farmington
Warwick
Dartmouth
Harwich
Wethersfield
New
Haven
Lyme
Falmouth
Yarmouth
Derby
Newport
Norwalk
Charlestown
Guilford
Saybrook
Stratford

***Early settlements concentrated along the Atlantic coast
and major Northeast rivers.***

do not mention the presence of stone walls. Nor were they of any real significance in most areas for the next hundred years. Jared Eliot's *Essays on Field Husbandry in New England* (1748 to 1760), the first treatise on agricultural practices in the British colonies—one that included detailed descriptions of how to enclose land, whether by fencing, ditching, plashing (integrating a mix of wood and hedge), or hedging—contains no mention of stone walls. Similarly, the anonymous *American Husbandry* (1775) comments extensively on both the purpose and the condition of colonial enclosures, but does not mention fences or walls made of stone.

Ironically, one of the first mentions of stone walls in the colonies is from an archaeological context. According to the historian Howard Russell, the failed Sagadahoc colony from 1607 had "left behind 'Rootes and Garden Hearbes and some old Walls' to be observed by a visitor a decade and a half later."[1] Apparently, they were first noticed not for their value as a building accessory, but as physical evidence of earlier human life, in this case the earliest English colonization in the Northeast.

Part of the explanation for the dearth of stone walls early on is cultural—the Pilgrims and the first generation of Puritans in the Massachusetts Bay Colony were agriculturists living a somewhat communal lifestyle. Another factor is resource based—wood for fencing was widely available, and not enough stone had yet accumulated on the surface of the soil. Most of the explanation, however, is geological. Successful plantations were established along the coast and its tidewater estuaries, and in river interval lands. These settings, which are distributed sporadically along the coast and large valleys, offered flat, well-drained topography adjacent to navigable rivers, a reliable source of freshwater, and a mantle of loamy soil. This is where the earliest settlements were begun, and where the colonists remained secure until hostilities with the Indians abated a few decades prior to the American Revolution. Hence, for the first century or more of settlement, movements of English settlers into the stone-dotted uplands were often restricted to the fringes of ancient coastal and river towns or to internal lands.

ဟ௭

ALTHOUGH PRIVATE PROPERTY DID EXIST, THE EARLIEST Puritan communities were highly regimented social colonies. The primary identity lay with the group, rather than with the individual, a pattern dating back to medieval times. This approach made good sense in a world where the settlers, clinging to the shore, looked out to see nothing "but a hidious and desolate wilderness, full of wild beasts and willd men," in the words of William Bradford, early governor of Plymouth Plantation. Some of the earliest settlers even had timber palisades around their village centers, which, at least psychologically, were not unlike those of European castle walls. From the village's defended center, the common folk swarmed out by day to work their fields, then returned at night, like bees to a hive.

Even without palisades, however, early colonial villages were always tightly knit and centered upon the church, which was both a place of worship as well as the seat of government. (Religious tolerance, particularly the constitutional separation of church and state, did not come for more than a century. How easy it is to forget that separation of church and state—something we take for granted—was an American, rather than a colonial, notion.)

Early village house lots often faced a single town street. They were large enough for a garden, but not for important agricultural work, which took place in communal enclosures where families worked their own plots of arable land. Livestock grazed together in meadows and marshes as part of a single herd, then were enclosed in a

Early Colonial Village (1640)

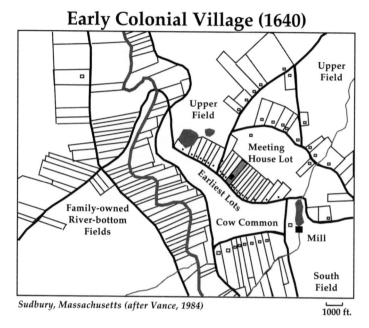

Upper Field

Upper Field

Meeting House Lot

Earliest Lots

Family-owned River-bottom Fields

Cow Common

Mill

South Field

Sudbury, Massachusetts (after Vance, 1984)

1000 ft.

Layout of a colonial village.

community fence at night. Plows and oxen teams were collectively owned and allocated.

The fences of early Puritan settlements were not designed to separate people from one another. They were agricultural devices used to enclose vegetable gardens, to protect cultivated fields from marauding livestock, and to shield domestic animals from the perils of the night forest, a chronic threat to livestock in seventeenth-century New England. The early Puritans experimented with Old World fencing techniques such as ditches and hedges. But nearly all of their successful fences were made of wooden pales;

long pieces of wood were driven downward into the earth and spaced closely together, a fencing technique that would later evolve into the white picket fence of today. Saplings, split in half lengthwise, were especially easy to convert into pales, and saplings were abundant in abandoned villages vacated by Indians because of epidemics of European germs, notably smallpox. The fencing off of large tracts of private property, first with wood, then much later with stone, was alien to the seventeenth-century Puritan mind-set. The same was true in parts of Britain at the time, much of which was then largely an unfenced pasture.

∽

THE NATIVE TRIBES OF NEW ENGLAND ALSO PLAYED AN IN-direct role in the delay of the appearance of stone walls on the New England landscape. Mohegan, Nipmuck Pequot, Narragansett, Penobscot, Pamasquoddy, and many other tribes had tolerated European—Dutch, British, Swedish—settlements during the first half of the seventeenth century. They even encouraged them when it suited their needs, especially when the settled "whites" formed an alliance against their enemies. The natives sometimes were genuinely helpful, as with the case of Squanto, the Indian who helped the Pilgrims survive their first winters and who was alleged to have been present at the first Thanksgiving feast.

By mid century, however, it had become painfully clear to the Indians that the "palefaces" were here to stay, were becoming more powerful every year, and were even capable of genocide; English colonists attempted to exterminate all of the Pequots on the Connecticut coast in the late 1630s. Concerned for their own survival, a confederacy of formerly unaligned tribes waged a series of raids in 1675 to 1676 that came to be known as King Phillip's War, named after the charismatic leader of the tribes. In a typical encounter, a farmer was ambushed in the fields, the cluster of buildings put under siege and burned, the children killed, the young women carried away, and the livestock slaughtered.

King Phillip's War was followed by nearly a century of conflict known as the French and Indian Wars, during which the shifting alliances between Indian tribes became caught up in the distant struggle between France and England for the right to rule North America. Hostilities finally ended with the Treaty of Paris in 1763, when France formally surrendered its claim to eastern Canada. Before that treaty, however, interior New England, especially to the north and west, was a danger zone ruled by tomahawks and flintlock muskets. Some of the most impregnable stone chambers, although originally constructed as storage sites such as root cellars, may instead have become fireproof fortifications against Indian raids.

The effect of native hostilities on New England's stone walls was to promote slow expansion of the original colonial settlements around their edges, rather than the founding of separate new ones, especially in the deep interior, far from the coast. Settlers who might otherwise have struck out to create new colonies in the wilderness instead remained in existing villages, crowded with their relatives, waiting for things to change. The delay caused by Indian hostilities coincided with, and reinforced, the delay caused by the lingering attractiveness of the river interval lands with their productive alluvial soils. Only after supremacy over the Indians and the British became assured, and only after the interval lands became full, would there be a burst of settlement in the wilderness.

ಌಌ

THE IDEOLOGICAL BREAKDOWN OF THE PURITAN CULTURE also contributed to the surge. According to John Hart in *The Rural Landscape,* "The original generation or two of Puritans were firm believers in original sin; they knew that they, themselves were wicked, and they assumed that everyone else must be just as sinful as they were." They knew that the community was strongest when everyone was kept "in the village because it was more difficult for people to misbehave when they were living side by side under constant surveillance. Those who lived on isolated farms were much more easily tempted to develop disrespect for authority, to indulge in strong language and stronger drink, and even to go so far as to accept bad weather and poor roads as excuses for failing to attend church on the Sabbath."[2]

"The New England clergyman wielded virtually sovereign power—an absolute monarch over his congregation," said Walter Blair, Theodore Hornberger, and Steward Randall in *The Literature of the United States.* As the late seventeenth and eighteenth centuries progressed, settlers increasingly asked themselves why they should live under repressive, centralized authority when fertile land free of savages lay to the north and west, ripe for the taking. Population growth contributed to the surge as well, along with a shift toward the pasturing of cattle for milk and beef.

Third- and fourth- generation Puritans, especially the young and restless, answered this call with their feet, moving inland from the coast and upward from tidal rivers toward the uninhabited interior where land was readily available. These sons and daughters launched the first great emigration from the ancestral colonies. The original seeds of settlement planted by the English in the coastal lowlands and interval lands had germinated successfully, and were now broadcasting seedling colonies in what had been, only a decade or two earlier, a "howling wilderness." These colonies would, a century later, broadcast another spawning of colonies to the American West.

While settlers were emigrating to the uplands of the New England Plateau, there were sweeping changes in land-use settlement patterns. Taverns began to replace churches as civic centers of influence. Towns were no longer laid out as islands in an otherwise unoccupied landscape, each a tight-knit community of like-minded souls. Instead, larger farms began to sprawl outward, away from established villages and along primitive roads. Individualism, which had always been an element, even in Puritan settlements, was on the rise.

Although some of the best arable land was still worked in common, especially by extended families, starting in the late 1600s farms were becoming independently owned and operated. Farmers became self-reliant in most things—defense, ownership, food, education, and technology—coming together primarily for spiritual reasons. This emigration to the inland plateau was American, rather than colonial in style, because it emphasized individual liberty rather than group cohesion, and self-sufficiency rather than export. From such inland farms would come the minutemen, whose values paved the way for American independence.

The shift from communal to individual land ownership and from densely populated villages to more isolated
farms was a critical step in the eventual spread of stone
walls over the landscape. This was the ideological force
that lifted the farmers, their tools, and their stock above
the stone-free lowlands, toward the lushly forested but
stone-rich uplands of the New England Plateau. Two factors—a sense of private property and soil on stony till—
critical to the proliferation of stone walls were now in
place. The third factor—the taking of the forest—was next
in line.

⌐⌐

THE PIONEER MOVING INTO THE NEW ENGLAND PLATEAU
during the early eighteenth century was not the romantic,
buckskin-clad frontiersman made famous by James
Fenimore Cooper in his *Leatherstocking Tales*. Instead he
was an ordinary farmer. A workingman with a wife and
children, one who lived a humble if not hardscrabble life.
In *American Myth and Reality*, the historian James
Robertson writes, "The pioneer brought oxen and other
draft animals to the frontier, pulling wagons and carts full
of civilized goods . . . expecting to build a house and barn,
to farm . . . to build a community . . . He was settling, and
he intended to put himself down and stay put."[3]

Rarely did a family settle alone in the wilderness;
rather, the establishment of towns was usually a corporate
event. Prior to the mid–eighteenth century, this often happened via the proprietorship system in which groups of
worthy men formed a township or town, often just inland
from those already established. Such like-minded groups
acted essentially as a franchise moving to a new location.

In other cases, fledgling towns wishing to grow in size—perhaps in order to justify the expense of a minister—offered the incentive of cheap, virtually free land, provided that settlers move in and "improve" (deforest) the forest. For example, Cornwall, Connecticut, in 1738 required that a settler clear and fence six acres within two years.[4] Towns often subdivided when the population became dense enough to support two congregations; this eliminated the arduous journey of those most distant souls to church on the Sabbath. Finally, there was a trend toward the granting of land to individuals of wealth or prominence, land which was then subdivided and sold at market value. Attracting new settlers was part of the deal. It raised the property values of the remaining unsold lots. Such market-driven speculation in real estate helped to ensure that the inland was settled rapidly. It has been part of America ever since.

"Improving" land from its wilderness condition took place in stages. First, locating and examining property usually took place during a horseback journey into the roadless forest, sometime after the relentless chores of the growing season had eased. Locating the exact boundaries of a tract, even for surveyors, was difficult because the straight-edged polygonal land divisions of British law (squares, rectangles, parallelograms, triangles) bore little, if any, relationship to the irregular and gradational shapes of nature, at least on the scale of farms. Horizontal distances, called bounds, had to be measured with a chain dragged between the trees. Compass directions, called metes, were referenced to objects like "the old butternut tree," whose identity could be mistaken and whose permanence could not be guaranteed. Secular variations in the Earth's magnetic field, which caused the compass to shift in the direction it pointed each year, were particularly dramatic during colonial times, adding further confusion to an already difficult surveying job. The urban clerks and attorneys who prepared deeds and titles had little appreciation of either these global trends or of woodland reality.

The next stage was exploration and planning for an eventual move. Hills and swamps had to be located and counted. Ledges and stony ground, if present, had to be avoided. The warmest, sunniest, flattest land had to be found for tillage. A home site had to be envisioned. Resources—timber, firewood, stone, water, game—had to be inventoried. A family graveyard had to be located because deaths, particularly of children, were a fact of pioneering life. And the number of children per family and town was staggering compared to modern times, even though many people lived to a ripe old age. The birth rates were simply much higher than the death rates. Social security came from one's children.

Monumentation—physically marking the land—was the next stage, being mandatory for legal possession. Trees were blazed with an ax, often with an identifying symbol, like X or an angled pair of slashes, / /. Cairns (postlike stacks of stone) were built along property edges, especially on rough land. A line of brush could be cut, or a row of cedar posts pounded in—whatever it took to claim the land. Corners were usually marked with a small pillar of stones, or by selecting a large elongated stone and setting it upright in the soil, like a primitive obelisk.

The Indian tribes had relied on the irregular geometry of nature—rivers, ridges, and coastlines—to delineate their territories, which bounded tribes instead of individuals. They used political influence and violence to maintain their territories. In contrast, pioneering English settlers were legally required to clearly define their property boundaries, which almost always had straight edges. Although tensions between adjacent farms were low at first, subsequent crowding produced powerful territorial antagonisms between neighboring properties. Such crowding was brought about by rising population, the sub-division of farms through generations of patriarchy, and speculation in rising land values. This tension would inaugurate the first stone "walls" of interior New England.

"Good fences make good neighbors." So claimed the poet Robert Frost in his most famous phrase, one that was borrowed from an earlier almanac, and which had been used to describe South Carolina.[5] Regardless, he knew that territorial tensions could be ameliorated with a clear expression of ownership. Hence, whenever possible, the lightly marked early boundaries—slashes on trees, small cairns of stones, wooden stakes—of the earliest pioneers were translated into permanent ones. If enough stone was available, a boundary "wall" would be built, often being little more than a knee-high stack of stone, like the one in Derry, New Hampshire, separating the poet from his neighbor. Such "walls" were neither livestock fences nor ornaments, but territorial markers made with stone. The poet and his neighbor walked "the line" each spring like wary foxes to repair their common boundary, ensuring that peace might prevail. (Humans are among the most territorial of all animals.)

Residual Puritan notions, handed down from the previous generations, were also factors underlying the urge to mark properties clearly, preferably with stone. The historian Peter Carroll writes: "Like most Puritan concepts, the social ideals transported to America reflected centuries of

***Photograph of a diorama depicting an early settler
clearing a homestead.***

Old World experience." They enclosed their communities
with "a protective wall which surrounded a people and assured them that the Lord would not forsake [them]."[6]
Thus, arranging stones in a line to mark the property edge
went beyond simple territorialism; it was an almost religious act for the eighteenth-century descendant of Puritan
thinking. Each line of stone unambiguously announced
the boundary between the righteousness of one farm and
the sinful chaos of the other; or between the good of the
human community against the evil of unimproved land.

Many stone walls standing in the woods today were thus
part of a "territorial imperative." Over the next two centuries—as more land was cleared and as more stone

accumulated in fields—these territorial markers were lengthened, straightened, emboldened, and embellished into ever more permanent "estate" walls of the late nineteenth century, which are essentially beautiful No-Trespassing signs written in stone. They had little, if anything, to do with agriculture.

～

AFTER MARKING PROPERTY BOUNDARIES, THE NEXT JOB FACing the pioneer was the most strenuous one. He had to clear-cut the forest, beginning with a place for the house, then moving outward in a widening swath through future farmyard and fields. Solitary trees were sometimes left for pasture shade. Otherwise the land was clear-cut, shaved of every tree and brush.

The forest encountered by the colonists was highly variable. The ecologists David Foster and John O'Keefe explain: "The pre-settlement landscape was not a stable, monotonous, unchanging forest. Rather, it showed considerable temporal and spatial variation in the mixture and distribution of species and the pattern of vegetation. An ongoing process of natural disturbance—by hurricanes, other windstorms, ice storms, pathogens, and fires ignited by lightning strikes—led to differences in the age, density, size and species of trees across a wide range of sites." To the north—from southern Maine to New Hampshire to Vermont—cooler, moister conditions had led to a northern hardwood-hemlock-white pine forest. In the transition zone to the south, "cool ravines, on north slopes, and at higher elevations favored the growth of 'northern' species, including hemlock, beech, yellow birch, sugar maple, poplar, red spruce, and balsam fir. More exposed and drier sites on ridges, well-drained soils, and to the south supported 'southern' species, including white, black, and scarlet oak, hickory, chestnut, black birch, and pitch pine. Intermediate sites were characterized by a mixture of both groups, and in addition by white pine, red oak, white ash, black cherry, and red maple."[7]

The strenuous, acute task of clear-cutting was done over a period of several long summers, followed by winters back home, where equipment could be gathered, axes sharpened, seeds gathered, and plans made for the day when permanent residency would begin. Three or four years was enough to make the transition between ownership and permanent occupancy.

In slow progression, patches of so-called improved land expanded outward from each farmstead until they intersected with similar patches on adjacent farms. In the heavily settled parts of southern and eastern New England, forested towns dotted with a few clearings were gradually transformed into cleared towns dotted with a few remaining forest patches. As part of this transformation, miles of roads—most of them terrible—were then bordered by fields and fences instead of by wilderness. Primitive stone walls were a natural consequence of road building because the stones, exposed to horse and wagon traffic and erosion, had to be moved aside.

By the middle of the nineteenth century, when deforestation reached its peak, more than half of New England's native forests—as much as 80 percent in the heavily settled parts of southern New England—had been cut down and replaced with "open space," meaning tillage, mow land (land used for hay cutting), and pasture. Deforestation reversed the ecological pattern of plant colonization that had taken place during the much earlier transition of New England's postglacial parkland to continuous forest.

Less than 10 percent of "improved" land was used for tillage fields put to the plow. Remaining lands were divided roughly equally into meadow for haying and high-quality pasture. Rough, cleared lands, called bushpasture, were used for grazing, and so-called unimproved land was left as managed woodlot or because the land might have been too rough to manage effectively. The proportions between these different uses varied somewhat between low-land and upland, but the presence of all five functions was part of a general pattern requiring the removal of trees.

Generally speaking, the original settlers used the forest composition—the species of trees—to determine what use to put the land to. For example, "sugar maple, beech, and ash grew on productive sites that were suitable for crops; chestnut and oak dominated the broad, moderately productive uplands that made good pastureland; and hemlock and red maple sites were usually wet rocky and less suitable for agriculture."[8]

Those patches of forest left uncut were not necessarily unscathed. Livestock, especially during the first decade of a farm's existence, grazed intensively in the forest, removing the understory and damaging the soils. Additionally, there was a heavy demand for wood as fuel and for fencing. Sugaring—the extraction and boiling of sap—was another activity that had an impact on the forest, even when the trees were left standing. Tanneries needed hemlock bark, stripped from dead trees. Potash, made from the ashes of burned wood, caused losses as well.

ဟၑ

THE METHODS OF FOREST CLEARING WERE SIMILAR ACROSS the region. Smaller saplings and shrubs were removed first, often by burning. Larger trees were often simply chopped down at waist level, especially if the land was needed as soon as possible. More often, they were girdled with an ax, a laborsaving process in which a ring of bark was stripped from the circumference of the trunk, killing the tree slowly, almost without effort. Stately trees, sometimes four hundred years old, died standing up, evolving into wooden skeletons whose limbs fell randomly and dangerously before they were finally cut down.

Many fallen trees, whether chopped or girdled, gave up their timber for houses, barns, and sheds. Settlers could make their own structural timber by sectioning and shaping trees into posts and beams. But sawmills, which performed this job more efficiently, sprang up in every foundling town.

Most trees were not destined for lumber. They were cut down, chopped or sawed into movable sections, wrapped in chains, and hauled into piles by a team of oxen. Although usually done slowly, sometimes this final phase of clearing became a festive neighborhood event known as a "logrolling," one not unlike that of a barn raising, during which the hard cider often flowed freely. Trees and stumps burned in huge, smoky fires that smoldered for weeks, similar to what is happening today in the Brazilian Amazon.

More rarely, specialized teams did deforestation. In the most well-planned, capital-intensive, corporate clearing projects, teams of workers handled different aspects of the job, following each other in phases. This tradition dates back to medieval Europe, where "one group (the incisores) cut down the trees, a second (extirpatores) took out the trunks, and a third (incensores) burned up the roots, boughs and undergrowth." This process was sometimes used in the most remote parts of Vermont and New Hampshire, when landowners or real estate speculators sometimes hired gangs of foresters. Their "only business [was] to cut down trees and open land for cultivation, build log houses and prepare the way for others."[9]

In southern maritime New England, especially near the large wealthy cities, slaves were used to clear the forest. For example, in Salem, in southeastern Connecticut, New London County, a wealthy man named Colonel Samuel Brown gradually bought up thirteen thousand acres of wooded land beginning in 1718, most of which had been Mohegan territory only a few generations earlier. Measuring nearly five miles by six miles square, he called it New Salem Plantation, modeling it after those of the South. He hired an "overseer and brought in 60 families of Africans—as many as 120 people—to clear the land."[10]

Something similar took place when landless groups of Native Americans were paid virtually nothing to clear land, or when prisoners, working as part of a chain gang, did it for free. However, these are exceptions to the general rule; most of the New England forest was cleared by the property owners and their seemingly countless numbers of children.

With the trees gone, the land was ready for pasture or seed, even if stumps remained. Early crops of grass and grain were sometimes put in before the land was plowed. First crops could be the best ones because the nutrients formerly locked up in the leaves and wood had been liberated by burning. Scenes of cows grazing around charred, rotting stumps or a farmer hoeing between them were common ones on pioneering plantations. After the roots had rotted sufficiently, the stumps were tipped out with a team of oxen and dragged to the edge of the field. There, they became integrated into the first fences, which were usually amorphous mixtures of brush, stumps, and small logs called poles, with a few stones thrown in for good measure.

With the stumps gone, and the dense mat of roots rotted away, the final stage was to prepare the land for cultivation by stock-drawn implements. Oxen were the preferred source of power. Timothy Dwight was fascinated by the process. He provides an eyewitness account from near Lake Winnipesaukee, New Hampshire, around the beginning of the nineteenth century.

> *After the field is burned over, his next business is to break it up. The instrument, employed for this purpose, is a large and strong harrow; here called a drag, with very stout iron teeth; resembling in its form the capital letter A. It is drawn over the surface, a sufficient number of times to make it mellow, and afterwards to cover the seed. A plough would here be of no use; as it would soon be broken to pieces by the roots of the trees.*[11]

Note that Dwight did not write "broken to pieces" by the stony ground in this scene from New Hampshire, later dubbed the Granite State. He so loved to detail the sufferings of pioneers that he would not have missed this perfect opportunity to disparage the stones had they been a significant problem at the time. Apparently, it wasn't the stones that might wreck a pioneer's plow, but the living roots of trees. As late as 1775, the widely used farming manual "American Husbandry" didn't concern itself with stony soils. As late as 1792, Governor Jeremy Belknap of New Hampshire mentioned that the mineral soil, which includes the stones, "does not appear till after the earth has been opened and cultivated." Indeed, there is a dearth of early remarks about stony soils.

It would be an exaggeration to suggest that stones were absent from early upland pioneering settlements. Erratic boulders would certainly have been visible in many places, and almost every upland farm had patches of stony ground from which stones were taken as resources used for building fireplaces, foundations, and cellars. But a plethora of evidence—eyewitness accounts, historic descriptions, modern soil maps, field investigations, the journal of Henry David Thoreau—indicate that the cumbersome abundance of stone on cleared lands came later.

ဆ

SINCE THE CULTURAL SHIFT TOWARD PRIVATIZATION OF property required the construction of miles of fences, as well as a way to regulate their effectiveness, fencing laws emerged. They set the specifications for different types of fences, levied fines for substandard barriers, and established the legal grounds on which neighbors could sue each other. Fencing laws were not passed capriciously. Keeping animals and crops apart was critical to the economic well-being of communities, and was thus the source of rancorous debate, especially in early town meetings. This was certainly true of the town of Mansfield, Connecticut, whose records indicate that fencing and animal trespass were discussed at nearly every town meeting between 1703 and 1853.[12]

Four types of wooden fencing (clockwise from top:
picket, board, zigzag, post-and-rail).

Public officials known as fence viewers were appointed to ensure that fencing ordinances were being followed. They understood that a low row of poles or stones was sufficient to guide cattle out to pasture but would not be expected to hold back a horny bull in rut. Similarly, fences between pastures could be lower than those keeping animals away from more tempting crops like corn. Highest of all, up to eight feet tall, were the walls of town pounds (animal jails), which held animals that had already tasted the "call of the wild." In general, however, the legal height of a fence in the colonies was between four and five feet. A substandard fence prevented a landowner from suing owners of wayward stock, and vice versa. Empirically, it had to be "sheep high, bull strong, and hog tight." The last criterion was the most demanding.

New England statutes still specify the appointment, jurisdiction, and duties of the fence viewer, although their power is much diminished and hardly noticed. But in the late colonial period, they would cruise rural land like the state troopers of today, looking for trouble and writing citations.

Most early barriers were "expedient fences," made from the refuse of the clearing operation. Stump fences, made by dragging stumps to the edge of the field with their severed trunks pointing outward, were widely used, especially in the drier, colder air of northern New England, where they would last for decades. Brush and boulders were used like caulking to plug the holes between the whorls of tree roots in order to make a continuous barrier. In many respects, stump fences were very similar to the famed hedgerows of southern Britain, because the tangle of woody roots was frequently overgrown with ivy and wild grapes. Thoreau indicated that a very few "turf" or sod walls were built by immigrant Irish in his native Concord, Massachusetts, but they soon rotted away.

Log fences were made by stacking logs one above the other, parallel to the edge of the field, using stakes to hold them in position. Pole fences were made using the trunks of small trees and saplings that were either propped into position with piles of rock or held up by an A-frame. The use of ditches, standard technology in Britain, worked well in the flat, sandy fields near the southern coast and in some fertile interval lands, but weren't worth the trouble of digging in the till-covered uplands. Hedges also failed because they required too much attention, and because imported hedge-forming species were ill adapted to New World plant diseases (blights and rusts) and insects. Plashing (weaving material horizontally between vertical poles) and wattle (an even tighter weave of finer materials) were used only near gardens. Wire fences would not exist for at least another century.

These early ad hoc fences were soon replaced by wooden ones. Progressive attention to aesthetic considerations played a role in this transition, but also important was the loss of raw materials left over from the clearing operation. There were several standard versions of wooden fence. Most common was a post-and-rail fence. A hole was dug into the ground and the post was planted. Stones pulled from the hole were used as part of the backfill or to prop up the post as extra support. Once the posts were in place, usually at intervals of ten to twelve feet, the rails were attached by inserting them into a carved slot, by pegging or nailing them to the post, or by binding the rails with strips of bark or cordage. Owing to its resistance to rot, the preferred wood for posts was cedar, which was usually harvested from swamps, during the winter. Chestnut was preferred for rails because it decomposed slowly and was easily split.

The zigzag fence, also called the worm fence or Virginia rail fence, worked well on rough ground because digging and attachment devices were unnecessary. Instead, fence panels were laid out in a zigzag fashion, so that the rails in one tier were stacked above those of the next; usually five or six rails were sufficient. Least common and most expensive was the board fence, which was constructed of rough timber cut into boards six to eight inches wide, then nailed to a post; more rarely, boards were woven between closely spaced posts. Picket fences were not used in agricultural fields.[13]

Stone walls, of course, made an excellent fence because there were no posts, rails, or boards to rot. But during the early stages of improvement on pioneering farms, there was seldom enough stone, and even less time for the construction of walls. The progressive nature of the stone buildup is well documented by twentieth-century scholars. The rural sociologist Michael Bell writes "[stone walls] . . . appeared over time and were built mostly wall by wall as the supply of labor and of stones worked up by frost and erosion permitted." The historian William Cronon wrote: "[Wood fences] were used until repeated plowing turned up the rocks from which New England's famed stone walls were finally built." The archaeologist Robert Sanford said, "Stone walls . . . are the effort of three or four generations of men and women, boys and girls."[14] Except as intentional boundary markers on very stony ground, stone walls were usually not an early pioneering phenomenon. Instead, they were associated with farms that had been in place for a while, as it took some time to grow a crop of stones.

5

COPIOUS STONE

THE REVOLUTIONARY WAR, A DEFINING EVENT IN American history, dragged along between 1776 and 1783, and its aftermath had an enormous impact on the New England landscape, especially with respect to its stone walls. Most directly, the protracted war drew thousands of young men away from farms, even if only for a few months. Left behind were women, children, the elderly, the infirm, and those unable to leave. Those who remained worked the land even harder in order to help sustain the war effort, provisioning the Continental militias with bacon, beef, cheese, corn, grain, cider, beans, cabbage, squash, and fruit, which was often shipped in the form of brandy.

During the war years, a long-term, future-oriented perspective on land management gave way to a short-term, present-oriented priority for survival. The die had been cast for liberty, and now there was no turning back. The acute effort of winning the war came at the expense of capital improvements, which were often put off. Maintenance was neglected and fences disintegrated. The soils became impoverished as their nutrients were drawn out by crops faster than they were replenished by the addition of manure. Allowing land to rest, or be fallow, was a luxury few farms could afford. Fieldstones accumulated in pastures faster than they could be hauled away.

Rural community life was forever changed by the war. The enormous war debt—which accumulated through lost taxes, higher prices for imported goods, armaments, soldiers' pay, war provisions, and destruction of property—was often paid off in new land rather than in Continental currency, which was hardly worth the paper it was printed on. Also available were large tracts of land abandoned, literally, by the Tories; these were appropriated in various ways, then sold to the sons and daughters of liberty.

After the war, veterans and their war-weary families moved into towns created scarcely a half-century earlier during the initial exodus from colonial coastal villages. During the next two or three decades, the new nation's mood turned optimistic. Birth rates picked up, expanding the population dramatically. Country congregations expanded, overfilling their pews. Parishes split down the middle along largely geographic lines, then, like living cells, divided again and again. This was especially true in the more settled parts of southern and coastal New England.

Prior to its industrialization during the mid–nineteenth century, New England had always been an exceptionally rural population. During the postwar (American Revolution) baby boom, it became an exceptionally young one as well. For example, by the turn of the nineteenth century, only 4 percent of Connecticut residents lived in cities; "every third person was a child younger than five years old; only one person in six was older than 45."[1] No matter how many mouths there were to feed, there were twice that number of hands ready to work the land and pick up the stones.

The British naval blockade during the Revolutionary War had cut off the flow of imported manufactured goods, especially metal ones. This precipitated the establishment of Yankee factories in places where hydropower was available, which was on nearly every moderate-size stream. Industries associated with iron manufacturing, shipbuilding, distilling, and packaging accelerated the pace of deforestation, which was already being intensified by the cutting of wood needed to repair war-torn fences and buildings. Progressive industrialization helped concentrate populations in mill villages, creating new local markets for food products. Agricultural prices doubled during the last decade of the eighteenth century, raising the value of rural land throughout settled New England.

ഇ

MILLIONS OF STONE WALLS WERE BUILT AFTER THE BEGINNING of the American Revolution between 1775 and 1825. Several important changes in rural society were responsible for what writer Susan Allport refers to as a "frenzy of wall building." First, the rapid pace of wall construction coincided with the time when the children of the postwar baby boom had grown old enough and strong enough to pick up stones. Surplus labor was also available during one of several postwar recessions. Freed slaves, landless farmers, debtors, groups of "tame" Indians, disabled war veterans, and the generally unemployed were put to work building stone walls. Second, the generally optimistic landowning farmers were self-reliant American citizens with the confidence to build a great nation, if necessary, one stone wall at a time. This epoch also broadly coincided with the Federalist period, a time when farming and animal husbandry became more scientific.

Founded on improvements in public education and greater literacy rates, agricultural societies and journals were established in every state between 1787 and 1794. The secular "bible" of this era was Sam Deane's 1790 dictionary (actually an encyclopedia), whose title speaks for itself: *The New England Farmer; or Georgical Dictionary. Containing a Compendious Account of the Ways and Methods in which the Important Art of Husbandry, In all its Various Branches, Is, or may be, Practised, to the Greatest Advantage, In this Country.*

But the primary reason for the spread of stone walls on the land during this period was a geological one. Processes operating within and below the soil had combined to produce enough stone so that it could be used to fence the land.

Environmental historians generally conclude that the switch from wood to stone fencing in the early nineteenth century was an economic decision caused by the shortage of wood. For example, David Foster and John O'Keefe, in describing central Massachusetts, near Petersham, assert that, by 1830, "wood was now too valuable to use for fencing, so the abundant stones were used instead." William Cronon provides a more complex view: "The final shift to stone walls was thus a way both of ending the labor cost of repeated fence construction and of conserving disappearing timber resources."

But the switch from wood to stone probably had more to do with the availability of stone than the scarcity of wood as a resource. There is no arguing that, as pioneering

***An 1838 view of the countryside near
Groton, Connecticut.***

plantations evolved into productive farms, the supply of
wood shrank steadily, especially that of chestnut and
cedar, the most desirable materials for fencing. But it is also
true that the supply of stone had been rising steadily.
Wood and stone, it seemed, were reciprocal resources. One
went up while the other went down. The supply of wood
was highest at the outset, before the first tree was cut.
Conversely, the supply of stone was highest at the end,
when the lands had been cleared the longest.

The initial drop in the availability of wood on the landscape was due primarily to forest clearing; whole trees
were burned simply to be rid of them. Later losses were
driven by the chronic need for heat energy to keep houses
and buildings warm, for boiling maple sap, for use in the
butchering of animals, and for washing. William Cronon es-

timated that an average Yankee household used thirty to forty cords of firewood per year, each measuring four feet high, four feet deep, and twenty feet long. At that rate, many farm woodlots would soon have been exhausted. Uninhabited areas beyond farming villages were cut over as well, their wood being sold as an export crop. (Even the Caribbean rum trade took wood from New England in the form of ship timber, kegs, and charcoal.) Thousands of acres were clear-cut and their logs skidded to the nearest stream, floated to navigable rivers, then shipped to New England cities, especially Boston, Providence, New London, New Haven, and New York, which had long since exhausted their local wood supplies. The city of New Haven alone consumed 7,500 full cords of wood in 1811.

Among other uses for wood, the making of "coal," the early American term for charcoal, took the greatest toll on New England forests at this time. Tens of thousands of acres, especially in the western highlands of Connecticut and Massachusetts, were cut for charcoal that was used in the blast furnaces of the early iron industry because iron refining required a hotter, more dependable fire than one produced by wood.[2] "Coal" was made by hauling at least an acre's worth of timber to one site, piling it up in a giant, low cone, then burning the pile slowly beneath a smothering cover. Deforestation caused by charcoal production ended largely before the middle of the nineteenth century, when "real" coal—chiefly Pennsylvania anthracite—could be imported by canal and railroad. The steamships and steam railroads to come would consume wood for fuel as well. New England was headed down the path of Britain, which had been largely deforested since medieval times.

A shift toward sheep farming in the late eighteenth

century also correlates with the construction of stone walls, many of which enclosed sheep. But there's more to the connection between sheep and stone walls than farmers containing their herds. Pastoral cultures in the Mediterranean—Italy, Greece, Albania, Cyprus, Palestine— had learned from experience just how damaging sheep and goats were on hillside land. Their narrow snouts, hard, cloven hooves, flexible lips, and strong teeth evolved for pulling plants out by their roots in rocky areas. There is an old joke that "New Hampshire raised sheep because only sheep had noses small enough to reach down between the rocks for wisps of grass." John Muir, founder of the Sierra Club, was so disgusted by their damaging habits that he dubbed them "woolly locusts." Sheep and stone walls go together not just because extra enclosures were needed, but primarily because the expanding flocks damaged the topsoil, which yielded a bumper harvest of stones.

Actually, stone walls made a poor fence for sheep, unless the wall was at least four and a half feet high and with almost vertical, if not overhanging, sides. Since all breeds of domestic sheep are descended from an ancestral herbivore whose very survival depended on climbing rock cliffs to escape predators, sheep feel quite at ease on stone, but are seriously intimidated by wooden barriers. In many cases, stone walls provided little more than a place for sheep to cavort, even for those strains purposely bred to have stubby legs. It is a rare sheep fence today that is made entirely of stone. Most have a strand or two of electrified wire.

လ၁

THE MOST IMPORTANT LINK BETWEEN DEFORESTATION AND stone walling, however, wasn't about wood, sheep, labor, technology, or even human volition. It had to do with changes in the soil caused by the absence of the forest itself. By drying out the surface, changing the pattern of snow cover, and reducing the insulating value of the topsoil, deforestation inaugurated a sequence of specific chemical, mechanical, and thermal processes that would inevitably make the soil stony.

The upland New England soils, almost all of which were developed on different types of glacial till, were particularly susceptible to these processes, much more so than either lowland sandy soils or those that were already quite rocky. This was because till soils were compacted *below* rather than *above* the surface and had a significant component of silt, rather than sand or clay. Such soils are especially prone to frost heaving because the hardpan layer at depth traps infiltrating moisture and the silt promotes its dispersal, making these soils freeze easily and deeply when the ground is exposed to cold winter winds.

Although it seems counterintuitive, snowfall—particularly if it arrives early in the winter—mitigates the effect of frost heaving. Snow normally insulates the soil from the cold atmosphere and locks away moisture that would otherwise have seeped into the soil, where it could freeze and expand. Timothy Dwight observed that forested land, even at the latitude of northern New Hampshire, remained frost-free for much of the winter. "A stick forced through the snow in the month of February enters the earth without difficulty: the snow falling so early as to prevent the frost from penetrating the earth to any depth, and dissolving the little which had previously existed." But unforested land, even at the latitude of southern New England, freezes deeply; Samuel Deane remarked that: "When the ground is bare, it commonly freezes to as great a depth as water does, which, in this country, is sometimes not less than 30 inches."

The importance of snow and mulch in regulating the depth of ground freezing has been confirmed by more than seven decades of continuous meteorological measurements at Hubbard Brook, New Hampshire, where the U.S. Forest Service maintains its most intensively monitored hydrologic research station in the northeastern woodlands. Since measurements began in the 1930s, forested plots in Hubbard Brook have seldom frozen deeper than a few inches, with the maximum depth of freezing (six inches) coming during the year with the least snow.[3] In contrast, the depth of frost beneath nearby lawns and golf courses—the closest analog to an upland pasture during the late eighteenth century—exceeds two feet during many years.

Intense freezing wasn't necessarily seen as a problem by early farmers. In fact, Samuel Deane saw it as a benefit to the soil. "I suspect that our severe frosts in winter may have a tendency to excite a degree of fermentation . . . For the heaving and settling of the soil will make some alteration in the disposition of its particles, and conduces to its imbibing more freely, snow water and rains, which contain food for plants."[4] Thus, he advised farmers to augment the freezing process by furrowing the soil deeply. This was accomplished by dragging a coarse, heavily loaded rake or cultivator in the soft soil, to produce a series of miniature ridges and valleys. This increased the contact area between the summer-warmed earth and the winter atmosphere, making the transfer of heat more effective. It also simultaneously helped shade and dry the soil. On the one hand, Sam Deane was correct, because freezing can help break up resistant clods of soils and create new voids for the infiltration of rain. But the benefits of freezing were skin deep; with the subsoil frozen and less permeable to the downward percolation of water, surface runoff and erosion were increased.

The more hostile winter climates of late-eighteenth- and early-nineteenth-century America also encouraged the ground to freeze deeply, just at the time when the land was most deforested.[5] Mean annual temperatures during the half century of most active wall building (1775 to 1825) were colder and more variable than those of the present century. Exceptionally cold winters were noted when General Washington was at Valley Forge (1777 to 1778); during the period 1783 to 1785, when crops were ruined by summer frosts; and in 1816, the Year without a Summer, following the volcanic eruption of Tambora in what is now called Indonesia. Mean annual precipitation in the Northeast was also generally lower, as well, resulting, at times, in drier winters with reduced snowfall.

A cold climate at this time was not restricted to the northeastern United States, or even the Northern Hemisphere. It was a global phenomenon, the culmination of the Little Ice Age, an interval that began about A.D. 1100, when the Vikings abandoned their New World settlements. The Little Ice Age accelerated about A.D. 1300, peaked near 1850, and ended as the nineteenth century drew to a close. It may be no coincidence that the most intense decades of wall building occurred during this protracted period of colder, more variable, and drier winters, conditions that would have worked together to accelerate the heaving of stones from the soil.

Writing in America's first scientific monograph on soils, Nathaniel Shaler understood more than a century ago that frost heaving, which brought stones *up*, counteracted the burial of the stones by organic processes, which took them *down*. "As we shall see . . . this action of the frost is directly the reverse of that brought about by the work of plant roots and burrowing animals, which tend to remove the soil from beneath stones and to accumulate material on the surface in such fashion as to bury the masses."[6]

Frost heaving begins when liquid water, held on to soil grains by surface tension, freezes. Ice takes up 9 percent more space than an equivalent volume of water, ensuring that the soil expands during freezing. Since water in liquid and vapor phases is attracted, via a process called diffusion, toward soil that is already frozen, moisture is drawn up and adds to the amount of ice in the subsoil. Also, each speck of ice at the contact points between soil grains acts like a bridge, cementing the enlarging mass into a single, rigid body rather than a flexible, granular solid.[7]

As the frost line migrates downward, it reaches the tops of stones before it reaches their bottoms. When the bond between frozen soil and the top part of each stone is strong enough, the stone rises, creating a small void space at its base. Unfortunately for farmers and gardeners, however, two details of this "frost-pull" process are not reversible during the spring, when the fully expanded soil thaws and collapses back to where it started. First, although the soil must freeze from the top down, some of the thawing must proceed from the base upward, because the subsoil always contains residual warmth. This allows the soil adjacent to the void to flow into it while the stone above it is still frozen fast in position. The second nonreversible process is incomplete settling, which takes place during the final stage of thaw, when the frozen mass of soil that lifted each stone melts, softens, and subsides downward. The uplifted stone descends normally until its descent is blocked by whatever fell or squeezed into the hole. Being unable to descend, the stone has no choice but to move upward, punching its way through the soil settling around it.

Viewed from the perspective of the soil surface, the stones are being heaved upward. But this is only an illusion. When viewed from any other fixed frame of reference—such as the center of the earth—it is the land that is settling downward. The stone is, surprisingly, stationary.

A separate frost-heave process, called frost push, is effective at a shallow depth, perhaps ten inches or less. In this case, the cold is conducted into the ground more efficiently through the stone than through the more porous and organic adjacent soil. Hence, the base of a stone reaches the freezing temperature before the adjacent soil, nucleating the growth of ice that can push the stone upward.

The small upward movements caused by frost heave, although usually minor (less than a quarter of an inch), happen during every freeze-thaw cycle. At the rate of a quarter inch per winter, frost-heaved stones are ratcheted upward several inches per decade until they punch through the top of the soil. That's fast enough to make a century-old farm stony, but slow and hidden enough so that the process causing the stone to accumulate will be poorly understood.

After they were "born," the dirt-covered stones were usually washed clean by spring rains, giving the added illusion that they appeared almost overnight. Yankee farmers called them New England potatoes because they appeared like magical crops in fields that had been picked clean the year before. Others thought the stones grew from Satan's seeds. Nathaniel Shaler, a geologist, was one of the few who knew what was actually taking place underground.

The U.S. Army Corps of Engineers Cold Regions Research and Engineering Laboratory (CRREL), in Hanover, New Hampshire, is famous for its controlled frost-heave experiments. Using giant soil tanks within even larger refrigerators in their laboratories, CRREL scientists have watched stones heave upward more than five millimeters (a fifth of an inch) per day. They have also shown that heaving is more rapid where there is some slope, which enhances void closure, and where the soil contains some silt and clay, which enhances the holding and wicking of moisture. They have also shown that the physical attributes of each stone (shape, smoothness, density, size) make a difference: Rough, granitic, slab-shaped stones move upward faster than smoother, smaller ones; stones buried more deeply move upward more slowly because freezing takes place from the top down, and because the weight of the overlying soil holds uplifting stones down more effectively.

Another frozen-ground process, called thaw consolidation, accounts for increased stones at the surface. It takes place when void spaces in the subsoil produced by roots and animal life are destroyed by freezing faster than new ones can be formed by plants and animals. Thaw consolidation permanently shrinks the volume of the soil, allowing the soil surface to descend downward onto the stones being "pulled" up from below.

The sequence of stone sizes and shapes that will appear in a Yankee pasture or field can actually be predicted from these frost-heaving experiments. Large erratics would already have been visible on the recently deforested surface. Slabs from the melt-out till would be next, because they heave most effectively. Then a mixture of slabs and cobbles—rounded stones intermediate in size, between that of a boulder and a pebble—would appear. Last to come up would be small, rounded pebbles. First there would have been few stones. Then the rate of new stones would have accelerated to a maximum, then decelerated more slowly. Eventually, only a few stones would rise.

Tillage, rather than pasture, would have intensified the process because the raw mineral soil is most exposed to winter's cold, freezing more often and more deeply. The same is true for heavily used pasture, when compared to less-worn-out pasture soil. All other things being equal, cultivation and heavy pasturing would have produced more stones, bigger stones, more rapidly arriving stones, and more rounded stones than less intensively used land. Land under protracted cultivation would have, in the final stages, produced copious loads of small, rounded stones ranging in size from bread loaves to rolls.[8] Burning over the land prior to cultivation would have helped trigger frost heaving because the light color of the wood ash would have helped to reflect weak early-winter sunlight before the snows of late winter could insulate the ground. Thus, clearing, burning, tilling, and grazing would have awakened the stones from their thousand-year slumber as if they were bears being roused from hibernation.

This pattern of stone arrival was witnessed during the nineteenth century by an educated farmer named Hoyt

Louis Agassiz

from New Canaan, Connecticut, with a good sense of humor.[9] He took the day off to give a speech at the sixth annual meeting of the Connecticut Board of Agriculture. In a technical session titled "Improving Rocky, Sandy, and Barren Land," he described how the frequency, size, and rate of stone production were related. "We found that after getting off the first crop of stone, there was another one underneath . . . and many times the second crop has been quite as large as the first one. Although perhaps the stones were not so large, yet there were enough more of them to make up the difference." Had Mr. Hoyt's stones kept coming at the same rate he witnessed during the first decade or two of clearing, similar areas of New England would now look like the floor of a bedrock quarry. Fortunately, the supply of stones was limited by its original concentration in the ablation-till layer, which lay above the hardpan and below the biologically fractionated fine-grained soil.

Louis Agassiz, a Swiss immigrant and one of America's most distinguished natural scientists of the nineteenth century, understood that the supply of stones heaving up from New England soils was finite, and would someday be exhausted. ". . . the ground has already been cleared to a great extent of its rocky fragments. . . . In the course of time they will, no doubt, disappear from the surface of this country, as they have done from that of Europe."[10] The passage of time proved him correct, for those New England farms that stayed in business after the Civil War saw the abundance of stone diminish; it still kept coming, but more slowly and erratically.

The pattern of stone arrival suggested by these laboratory studies of frost heave, eyewitness accounts, comparisons with Europe, and contemporary predictions is that during the early years on pioneering homesteads there were few stones to be moved from pastures except for the largest. Within a few decades, however, stones began to arrive dramatically from their underground reservoir, making the clearing of stone an integral part of annual chores. Eventually, perhaps after a half century on tillage lands and a century of heavily used pasture, new stones declined as the supply from below was used up; those that could move had already done so.

Frost heave was not the only process responsible for concentrating stone. Loss of the topsoil through poor farming practices was another important factor. Cleared forest soils literally shrank in volume as the organic matter within them disappeared. Normally, under forested or grassland conditions, organic matter is added to the soil at the same rate it is extracted, and is recycled continuously among growing plants, the litter of leaves and twigs, and the topsoil. On farms, however, there is a net loss of organic matter because the biomass is physically removed through the harvesting of crops. This wasn't a problem until the volume of organic material in the soil, which had been accumulating for thousands of years, became depleted below some critical threshold. At this point, mulch or manure had to be brought in to maintain sufficient organic material and the limiting nutrients like phosphorus and nitrogen. Manure could be, and often was, hauled to fields in wagons. However, it was easiest to import manure by penning the stock, feeding them hay, and letting the "black gold" fall where it might. Manure was so important to agriculture that it was stored in barns to protect it from being leached by rainfall.

Soil erosion or the physical *removal* of topsoil took place wherever the mineral soil was exposed but not deeply plowed, and where it was compacted, either in response to declining fertility or by livestock trampling it. The chief factor responsible for producing surface runoff was the fact that the ground was frozen more often and more deeply, creating a barrier to downward infiltration of snowmelt and spring rains. The worst-case scenario for surface erosion took place when a thick snowfall came late in the winter on land that had been grazed too intensively. If melt took place quickly, the water locked up in snow acted like a bullet in a loaded gun about to be triggered by warm spring rains. Runoff was a much less serious problem in late summer and early fall, when tropical storms and hurricanes struck the region.[11]

Cobble in a pasture with a stone wall in the background.

The "top-down" mechanisms of soil loss (reduction in mass, compaction, and overland erosion) brought the surface of the soil, inch by inch, downward onto the stones rising up from below. When these two surfaces met, and when the stones weren't hauled away, the ground surface transformed itself into a cobble. Such cobbles today are often concentrated in the corners of old fields because livestock, particularly horses, tend to cluster in the corners where they nibble the vegetation down to nothing, soften the surface mud by stepping around in it, and compact the subsoil with their hooves, reducing its infiltration capacity. When the inevitable rainstorm finally occurs, water collects on the surface and runs off in sheets. This washes away the soft, stirred-up material at the top, concentrating the stones into a cobble. Today we use the term "cobble" to describe a large pebble or small boulder, rather than a patch of stony ground. The colonial cobblestone street is thus a copy of a naturally formed landscape element.

᪐

THE EROSION OF UPLAND SOILS BY COLONIAL AND THEN Yankee farming, and the stone walls that resulted, is well illustrated by a study in the village of Lebanon, in east-central Connecticut, just inland from the coastal town of Norwich.[12] Hilly terrain, originally mantled with typically loamy soil, Lebanon was occupied by the Mohegans before being deeded to a collective of colonists in 1692. Founding of the town, with 350 settlers, took place in 1695. As early as 1711, there were cattle drives to Boston, indicating that a pasture-based economy was already in place. Water management associated with dams and mills began shortly thereafter. The road network was essentially complete by 1734. By 1796, and with the population already in decline, there were more than 13,700 acres of cattle pasture on the town's tax list. Lebanon peaked earlier than most New England towns.

Topsoil washed downhill from pasture and tillage soils overwhelmed nearly every small hollow at the heads of streams. Countless small valleys below the hollows were converted to swamps, the drainage having been worsened by sedimentation. The small, perennial streams draining the swamps had their beds raised as much as six feet in the seventeenth and eighteenth centuries, creating broad floodplains that were ditched and drained as colonial mowing grounds. Intensified annual floods caused several small ponds and marshes to be completely filled by mud. The bottomlands of Lebanon and thousands of places like it in southern New England were effectively created during the colonial and Yankee eras as sediment washed off pastures and fields.

During intensive use of Lebanon's land for grazing and farming, the soil at the surface changed almost everywhere. The lowlands filled up with sediment washed off slopes, whereas the slopes became stonier, promulgating the construction of walls. Today, there are more drylands (walls and cobbles) and wetlands (filled valleys) than there were before people got involved. Both have evolved from a once more uniformly distributed thicker soil. The land, however, is not degraded. Instead, it is more ecologically diverse, more lived upon, more like that of Britain.

ᴄᴏᴊ

SEEMINGLY WANTON DESTRUCTION OF SOIL GREATLY CONcerned early European travelers, who, after living for centuries in one place, knew that soil needed careful attention. The eighteenth-century Swedish naturalist Peter Kalm was particularly appalled:

> *After the inhabitants have converted a tract of land into a tillable field, which has been a forest for many centuries, and which consequently has a very fine soil, the colonists use it as such as long as it will bear any crops; and when it ceases to bear any, they turn it into pastures for the cattle, and take grain fields in another place, where rich black soil can be found ... But the depth and richness of the soil found here by the English settler misled them, and made them careless husbandmen.*[13]

Illustration of an early plow.

By shifting around the location of tillage plots and pasture, New England farmers practiced something similar to swidden (also called slash and burn) agriculture, a technology usually associated with the notoriously poor soils of tropical rainforests, and which presupposes abandonment after a few years of use. Sometimes the American practice of abandoning one field for another went by the euphemism of "crop rotation," in which forest was taken for cropland, then given over to hay field, then to cow pasture, and finally to sheep range as its nutrient status declined. Some stony lands went through this sequence rapidly, being abandoned before their stones could be cleared away.

The plow is given far too much credit for bringing stones to the surface. A Vermont historical archaeologist recites the conventional wisdom: "When the land began to be plowed for fields, and the plow heaved up rocks, the problem of permanent fences was solved and . . . and New England's famed stone walls were begun." A more accurate view of the relationship between plowing and stone walling is provided by the ecologist David Foster: "These massive walls surround former cultivated fields where the collection of stones following plowing was an annual activity for all farmers, who added to and continually shaped these walls over long periods of time and through repeated years of use."[14]

Plows (then spelled "ploughs") did reveal stone in Yankee fields, but primarily because they penetrated slightly deeper into the soil than did the teeth of harrows, or the tread of human boots. But frost heave and other geological processes explain why farmers continued to find stones in fields that had not been plowed for years, and why stones showed up in places that had never been plowed. The exaggerated connection between stone and plow is retold through the generations because of its powerful symbolism; the stone, representing wilderness, confronts progress, the glistening plow. What actually happened is more interesting and ethically neutral.

ഇരു

ALTHOUGH STONE WALLS WERE BEING BUILT NEARLY EVERY-where in the half century after the American Revolution, they continued to receive little attention in farming manuals or in literature. For example, the longest statement on stone walls in Sam Deane's 1792 encyclopedia merely recommended using "stone of the slaty kind rather than pebbles [rounded stones], which . . . are a greater annoyance on a farm, as they need removing, but are not very good for any kind of building." The Reverend Peter Whitney, in his 1793 account—*A History of Worcester County in the Commonwealth of Massachusetts: with a particular account of every town from its first settlement to the present time; including its ecclesiastical state, together with a ge-*

Men with oxen team clearing a large boulder.

ographical description of the same. To which is prefixed, a map of the country at large, from actual survey—mentions the use of stones as a fencing material in a few of the four dozen "townes," but has nothing more to say on the subject.

Inattention to stone walls is also illustrated by Timothy Dwight's *Travels in New England and New York* (1821), a comprehensive and educated view of rural New England written when the upland pastures had been worked for at least a generation, and when stone was much more noticeable. In thousands of pages he occasionally mentions the presence of a stone wall, but provides only one full paragraph on the subject in his three-volume opus. In this paragraph, he describes the drumlin landscape between Pomfret, Connecticut, and Worcester, Massachusetts:

An eye accustomed to the beautiful hedges of England would probably regard these [stone] enclosures with little pleasure ... A great part of what we call beauty arises from the fitness of means to their end. This relative beauty these enclosures certainly possess, for they are effectual, strong, and durable ... Indeed, where the stones have a smooth, regular face, and are skillfully laid in an exact line with a true front, the wall independently of this consideration becomes neat and agreeable. A farm well surrounded and divided by good stone walls presents to my mind, irresistibly, the image of tidy, skillful, profitable agriculture, and promises to me within doors the still more agreeable prospect of plenty and prosperity.[15]

Reverend Dwight apparently could overlook the "rudeness" of stone walls only when they were put to use, and only when flat stones were "skillfully laid in an exact line with a true front." Almost everyone else, notably Ezra Stiles, in his commentary on his native Cornwall, Connecticut, focused on the bad side of the phenomenon:

Nature
Out of her boundless store,
Threw rocks together
And did no more.[16]

During the earliest years on farmsteads, stone was often heaped into piles, dumped in swamps, or stacked on ledges. Most of the stones moved during this stage were "two-handers," meaning that both hands were required to lift them. "One-handers" were usually ignored because they didn't interfere with the manually operated technology of the day, which was dominated by scythes for cutting grain and hay, shovels for digging, and separate forks for pitching hay and manure. Additionally, conventional wisdom held that small stones helped make soil more fertile. Some farmers actually worried that they would deplete the soil by taking too many of its stones away.

An exceptionally heavy stone or a load of smaller ones justified the use of a stock-drawn vehicle. A cart worked well on the firm ground of open pastures. On the rougher terrain of land being cleared, or on the softer terrain of cultivated fields, especially in spring, a stout wooden sled called a stone boat, or drogue, was used. Made of flat-bottomed timbers bolted together, a stone boat was yoked to a team of oxen, attached to a whiffle tree (a device for distributing the force between the chains), loaded with stone, skidded to the edge of a field, and off-loaded. Such work was often done during slack times, which was after harvests but before the ground was frozen, or during the interval between spring thaw and spring planting, when new stones were most visible.

Stone piles in the middle of pastures and fields were common during the first few decades of farming, and many still exist in the woods, especially on farms that were abandoned early on. But after a generation or two of farmers and their progeny, the edges of fields became the dumping ground of choice because the swath of land on either side of the fence had already been taken out of production; in this regard, the fence line was like a magnet for stone. At first, the stone was merely dumped in the weedy corridor, perhaps between the stumps of a brush fence, the rails of a worm fence, or the postholes. But eventually, so much stone accumulated that it was best managed by stacking it crudely, in order to conserve field space. This gave rise, almost automatically, to what is often called a tossed wall, in contrast to one that was fitted together, or laid. As they lengthened, individual segments of tossed wall would merge, a process that continued until entire fields were enclosed by a rough rim of stone. Thousands of "tossed" wall enclosures still survive.

To classify walls, it is important to make a distinction between the function of a wall and its structure. Functional walls include the retaining wall, the boundary wall, the estate wall, the stone fence, cattle guides, pens, foundation walls, cellar walls, and even walking walls, whose broad capstones were laid flat, like a sidewalk. Wall structure includes the single stack, in which large, often irregularly shaped stones are placed one upon the other; the double wall, in which slabby stones are slanted inward from two sides; and the disposal wall, in which two single walls are built several feet apart and the gap between them in-filled with stone. The degree of care with which a wall was built is also used to classify them. Dumped walls are those where the stones were randomly dumped. Tossed walls were given slight attention as individual stones were tossed into position. In laid walls, great care was given to selecting the stones and fitting them into an aesthetically pleasing "weave." Chinked walls had large gaps between the stones plugged with well-chosen or hammer-shaped smaller stone. Mosaic walls are those where large and small stones or dark and light stones were placed in a regular, often geometric arrangement. Copestone walls are those where the top tier of stone is laid on edge, rather than parallel to the ground surface.

The ecologist David Foster, having seen thousands of walls in Harvard Forest, distills all wall form, structure, and function down into two basic forms:

> *Broadly speaking, there are two predominant types of stone walls. "Single" walls consist of simple lines of typically large stones that usually enclosed pasture land. Since these fences served primarily to contain livestock and to separate lands of different use and ownership, farmers seldom bothered to construct them in elaborate form or in size beyond that demanded by their limited functional need. A second, much broader "double" stone wall often consists of well-formed parallel lines of larger stones with the intervening space filled with many small stones. These massive walls surround cultivated fields.*[17]

The vast majority of walls in New England are "tossed" walls, taking on either the "single" wall type—built around pastures for the expedient combination of stone disposal and fencing—or poorly built double walls. Most were initially viewed as quite ugly, especially by European visitors, who, according to landscape historian John Stilgoe, "disliked the stone walls because they seemed—and often were—poorly planned and poorly layered, liable to topple at the first frost, and certainly wasteful of space." Americans were not too proud of them either. Timothy Dwight apologized for their ugliness. Jess Buel, a widely regarded early agricultural reformer, recommended eliminating walls because they were of no value other than as a place to put the worst "obstructions to cultivation." The Reverend Dana Huntington wrote from his eastern Connecticut parish, "The land is deformed by immense craggy rocks . . . tottering stone walls with crooks and angles every few rods which rarely fail to attract the traveler unpleasantly." The historian Harold Fisher Wilson noted that "the stone walls and rail fences which outline [the fields]—they cannot by any stretch of the imagination be said to enclose them." In his 1939 book *The Stone Industries,* the mining engineer Oliver Bowles seems to have contemplated "strip-mining" stone walls as linear quarries, an action that speaks volumes about how he viewed them aesthetically.

The abundance of "tossed" (a.k.a., single) walls relative to laid walls is clearly explained by John Stilgoe:

> *The stone walls of New England . . . were built by men interested far more in land-clearing than in fencing. They piled the rocks not in heaps but in rows equidistant from the center of their rectangular fields, along each edge. As with so many other features of the American farmland, the [European] travelers misread the significance of the walls. American husbandmen looked not at ragged walls or at stumps or girdled tress. Instead they focused on the emerging rock- and stump-free fields they called arable.*[18]

Single wall (top); double wall (bottom).

Early fieldstone walls—those built before and shortly after the American Revolution on upland plateau farms— were ugly. Few were fences, either. Instead, they were primarily linear landfills, composed of nonbiodegradable refuse that was attracted to the edges of fields, as iron dust is to a magnet. Even Eric Sloane, who was reverent about all things colonial and early American, acknowledged that the walls were "little more than stones cleared from the fields that were piled neatly along one side." A century later, however, these stone dumping grounds would be appropriated as symbols of a vanished world.

ᒐᒧ

TERRAIN WITHOUT STONE WALLS DOES NOT MEAN THAT THE land was never farmed. Instead, it says more about the geological processes that may have buried the stones—as much as several hundred feet beneath glacial lake sediments—than it does about human activity. Conversely, a land parcel with massive, closely spaced walls says more about the thickness of the ablation-till layer than it does about cultural practices or the intensity of the farm effort. Henry David Thoreau might have been the first to understand how geological factors influence the location and layout of stone walls—in this case, in the hills of north Concord:

> *Excepting those fences which are mere boundaries of individual property, the walker can generally perceive the reason for those [stone walls] which he is obliged to get over. This wall runs along just on the edge of the hill and following all its windings, to sepa-*

> *rate the more level and cultivatable summit*
> *from the slope, which is only fit for pasture or*
> *wood-lot, and that other wall below divides*
> *the pasture or wood-lot from the richer low*
> *grass ground or potato-field, etc. Even these*
> *crooked walls are not always unaccountable*
> *and lawless.*[19]

The pattern he recognized—separate lines of walls following the contours at high and low elevations—is governed by geology. The gracefully curved lodgment-till hilltops of the New England Plateau usually lack a thick cover of ablation till. Hence, there are fewer and more irregular boulders and their corners are often battered into smoothness. Stone walls there are usually well built, spaced farther apart, straighter in line, and less massive than those farther downhill, where the ablation till thickens, and becomes more discontinuous.

At middle elevations, the pattern is more complex. There, rain and snowmelt from highlands washed downward, where it merged with glacier water moving toward the sea; this produced torrential stream flow that washed away the till, leaving dense concentrations of stone. It is in these middle elevations that bedrock ledges are most common, giant erratic boulders are frequent, and where massive boundary walls are common, in part because there was so much stone so early.

At the lowest elevations, in small valleys, walls are often absent because they are buried by sand and gravel. If present, however, they are usually poorly built and substantially collapsed because the stones and boulders from which they were made are rounded, and therefore less stable to stack. They were of the "pebbly kind" rather than the "slaty kind," using the terminology of Samuel Deane.

Geographic location within New England, rather than elevation, also controls the abundance and style of stone walls. Boulders near coastal headlands, extending from Staten Island in New York to easternmost Maine, are generally rounded, having the shape of deformed cannonballs in some places, baking potatoes in others. Conversely, walls well away from the coast, in the granite highlands of New Hampshire and inland Maine, are often built of large, straight-edged, almost diamond-shaped stones because that is the way the homogeneous rock fractured after it solidified underground.

The spacing of walls and the way they are put together also is linked to the bedrock and the glacial geology. Excluding sediment-covered interval lands and lowlands, walls are most rare, and often most poorly built, on the terminal moraine of the southeastern fringe of New England. There, on the islands from Nantucket to Staten Island, the "bedrock" is composed of weakly cemented sandy strata rather than tough metamorphic and igneous rock; essentially, the strata of the coastal plain are too weak to produce boulders. Also, by the time the ice sheet reached the islands, nearly all of the stones within it had either been incorporated into the till or crushed to oblivion. The rounded stones that did survive the trip were diluted by the abundant sand. Hence, any walls built there were made with as few stones as possible, balanced precariously upon one other. Residents call them lace walls because they are made as much of air as of stones.[20]

This regional variant contrasts with the extremely dense concentration of well-made walls in places like

Fairfield County, Connecticut, and Westchester County, New York. There the bedrock was tightly foliated, the glacier held a high concentration of basal debris, and there was little opportunity for meltwater reworking. Consequently, the walls there are massive, exceptionally stable, and well laid. They provide quite a contrast with the lace walls; they are impossible to see through. The difference in the pattern of stone walls from one region to the other doesn't reflect cultural choice as much as it does the abundance of granite over schist, whether the ice sheet was frozen to its bed, and how much meltwater was available.

The color of stone is also controlled by the geology. Near the edge of the Connecticut River Valley, the stones have the rich brick-red to maroon-brown color of the Jurassic deserts in which they were deposited; these were rocks from the rift basin. In Vermont, black slate is infused with white quartz veins, giving some of its walls a zebralike appearance; these were rocks from Iapetos. Walls in southeastern Connecticut and Rhode Island are pinkish, owing to the abundance of rose-colored feldspars in its granite; these are the ancient rocks of Avalonia. Large areas of northeastern Connecticut and central Massachusetts contain rocks that are rich in iron-bearing sulfurous minerals (pyrite, pyrrhotite, chalcopyrite) that rust strongly when exposed to the air, giving rise to yellowish-red stains that drip downward on the surface of otherwise light-colored rock; even quartz boulders are tinted orange. Most of the walls north of Narragansett Bay, Rhode Island, are dark gray in color, the neutral hue of the dirty, volcanic, sedimentary sandstone from which they were built. These walls sometimes contain fragments of coal and blackened fragments of plant fossils, speckling the otherwise dull color.

Stones throughout the region may be marked in curious ways. Flatirons are faceted stones, generally with a distinct flat face on one side. Such stones, after being tumbled about at the base of the glacier, were subsequently held firmly in place as they were ground down against smooth ledge, something similar to what happens when a stub of playground chalk is rubbed against a sidewalk. Some stones are drumlin shaped, smoothed on only one side. They were probably lodged in the till and held in place so firmly that their tops were eroded into egg shapes by the ice moving over them; their undersides remained flat or rough because the ice couldn't get at them. Other stones are bullet shaped, rounded on one end and flat on the other. They were made when a stone in the process of being pecked smooth by stone collisions was broken in half by something larger and harder. Scratches and gouges are most common on homogeneous, dark, soft rock such as argillite, which is essentially hardened mudstone.

The hardest boulders in New England, those made of tan-colored quartzite, are often highly polished because they traveled long distances at the muddy contact between ice and rock, yet could not be broken. They frequently have crescent-shaped impact scars resembling the "smiles" on a poorly hit golf ball. Each smile records a powerful but nonlethal collision near the top of the accreting till layer. Sometimes a whole sequence of closely spaced crescentic fractures are lined up in a row, either on the bedrock or on a far-traveled stone. These are called chattermarks. Each records a slight jerk, accompanied by a tiny earthquake, as two very hard rocks slid by each other incrementally. Something similar happens when a heavy

**Unusual marks on fieldstone, caused by weathering
and glacial scratching.**

piece of furniture is moved across the floor, its leg lurching
audibly in tiny jerks—slip, stick, slip, stick, slip, stick . . .

Perhaps the most curious of all markings on stones are
the straight, deep, narrow gouges. These marks often narrow in one direction or the other, or are parallel, or intersect at odd angles. The pattern looks like cuneiform script.
Although these stones have been interpreted by antiquarians and amateur archaeologists to be ancient inscriptions,
they merely record the erratic passage of a stone slab over
hard, rough rock. Each gouge signals a point of contact and
the passage of stone in a straight direction; a mark's
change in direction records a shift in the direction of the
stone being inscribed by the ice.

Stone walls say so much about the past. The geological thread of their history determined where stone walls

would be built, and how the pieces would fit together. The historic thread determined the specific location and form of each wall. But something else was needed to turn copious stone into the ubiquitous stone walls of New England. Required was a greater share of prosperity and available labor.

6

BUILDING WALLS

AMERICAN FARMING EXPERIENCED A GREAT metamorphosis during the first few decades of the nineteenth century. Prior to that time, farming was largely a semisubsistence activity in which food and fiber grown on farms were used there as well. Things like tea and teakettles were imported, whereas things like cheese and beef were exported in limited quantities. The need to "shop in town" was so weak that itinerant peddlers, hauling their wares from door to distant door, became a commercial success.

Subsistence farms were still being established at the turn of the century in the rough country far from colonial villages, especially in Vermont, New Hampshire, and Maine. But farming towns to the south, especially near nascent industrial cities, began to export more and more—vegetable produce, dairy products, and poultry—to an enlarging urban market. The roads were still quite terrible, scarcely passable with more than a slow wagon. Under this circumstance, products that could be most easily carried to market—those that had the highest value per unit of weight—made the best profits. The alternative was forcing the animals to "walk" themselves to market and

***Stone-faced dam for a clover mill at
Schoolhouse Brook Park.***

made even more sense. In this case, those animals with the
largest weight per unit were the most profitable. Yankee
drovers goaded their products toward principal cities
from the most remote corners of New England, leaving
great clouds of dust in dry weather, mired, impassable,
manure-blessed ribbons of mud in wet. They were the first
authentic American cowboys.

Regional specialty crops also emerged, notably wool
from Vermont, cranberries from the sandy bogs of Cape
Cod, hops from near Boston, cheese from the Berkshire
hills, and tobacco and onions from the Connecticut River
Valley.

The British trade embargo of 1808 and high tariffs on
imported goods after the War of 1812 stimulated those
manufacturing enterprises that were already present on a
small scale. Yankee industry flourished as it specialized

and increased in scale; shoes were made in one place, clocks, axes, gunpowder, pistols, etc., in another.

Without imported British wool, sheep farming exploded in popularity, leading to the growth of textile mills that would eventually make southern New England the cloth-manufacturing capital of the world. High tariffs on iron tools also stimulated a tool-making industrial culture centered in Worcester, Massachusetts. Agricultural by-products, particularly leather, precipitated the tanneries and shoemaking factories that would make Lynn, Massachusetts, world famous. All of these urban workers required that food be driven to them; market roads radiated outward from the densely populated mill cities like the spokes on a wheel.

The success of these "mill" industries had much to do with the geology of New England. Mills could be profitably "seated" only in narrow, constricted sections of streams, usually where a perennial stream was flanked by bedrock. Many other well-watered regions have sufficient water but lack a solid bedrock valley, having broad, winding, muddy channels instead. Although streams in drier regions often have the requisite bedrock channels, they lack the continuous flow of water. But New England has thousands of sites where both criteria are met. The uplift of the plateau had forced the streams to cut bedrock valleys that were narrow where the rocks were hard and wide where they were less resistant. It was the copious fill of well-washed sand and gravel in the broader reaches of valleys that created the aquifers that absorbed spring floodwater and released it more slowly all year, ensuring an adequate flow to industry.[1] Countless dams, all of which needed stone facing, appeared all over New

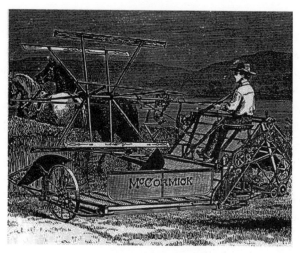

McCormick reaper and mower.

England at this time, taking some of the waste stone previously stored in crude walls.

Farming became a more technical, commercial enterprise in the nineteenth century. Nitrate, or guano (seabird excrement), from the Atacama dessert—then in Bolivia, now in northern Chile—was available to fertilize crops depleted of nitrogen. Something they called "plaister of paris," now known as the mineral gypsum, provided sulfur, which was needed to make plant proteins. It was imported from all over the world. Lime, made of calcium carbonate, was bagged and hauled in wagons to neutralize acidity; oyster shells were an inexpensive source of lime. Potash production—the making of potassium salts and oxides for fertilizer use—surged; farmers who still had plenty of wood started small "pot-ash" factories.

The tools of farming changed as well.[2] Implements for every task became more mechanized, automated, laborsaving. For example, the horse-drawn hay rake became widespread in the 1820s; before that, hay was gathered by hand. In the 1830s came multibottomed metal plows and specialized seed drills. These developments culminated in Cyrus McCormick's mechanical reaper, first marketed in 1834. With so many changes, agriculture was becoming less a way of life than a specialized trade taught at the college level; the first agricultural college, the Dariner Lyceum in Gardiner, Maine, opened in 1822. Specialty trade journals for eastern farming were published, notably the *American Farmer* (1819) and the *Albany Cultivator* (1834).

ಬಋ

THE SWITCH FROM SELF-SUFFICIENT TO MARKET FARMING took place when America was still a largely rural, agricultural nation, its people spread out all over the land surface on freeholding farms. It was an era of improvement and optimism, one without parallel in our history. The rapid urban growth of eastern cities fueled the demand for agricultural products, raising commodity prices and producing a broadly distributed pattern of wealth for rural New England farmers that would never come again. Yankee Sturbridge Village—a living museum in Sturbridge, Massachusetts, in the heart of the New England Plateau—captures the good times of the late 1820s and early 1830s. In 1825, the great New England orator Daniel Webster intoned, "Our proper business is improvement. Let our age be the age of improvement. In a day of peace, let us advance the arts of people and the works of peace."[3]

Tens of thousands of stone walls were built during this era of stable population, peace, and prosperity. Labor was available, there were no wars to fight, and the draining effort of deforesting the New England Plateau had been largely expended. Farmers throughout the region began to look inward at their farms, not as safe havens from war, but out of pride in being an American. A visible manifestation of this pride was the transformation of stone piles and primitive field-edge tossed walls into classical double walls that once surrounded productive farms, but which now thread their way through our woodlands. This didn't happen all at once, nor did it happen at the same time in all districts. In fact, some farms, such as the slave-operated estates in Rhode Island, had well-built stone walls from nearly the beginning. But in general, the primitive tossed walls and stone accumulations of the preceding epoch were either built up and leveled off or disassembled and rebuilt into their well-ordered early- to mid-nineteenth-century counterparts.

How such crews went about upgrading walls was seldom described. At least two men, a team of oxen, and a stone boat were typically used. The labor involved in such a transformation was extremely high. Modern masons often lay about twenty feet per day. An expert on British walls, Lawrence Garner, estimates that a good "waller" there can lay 5 to 6 yards a day. The agricultural historian Howard Russell concludes that "a good man with a good team might build four rods a day," or sixty-four feet of basic New England wall. Using the average of these estimates for the rate of wall construction and the estimated length of New England's stone walls from the 1871 fencing census (240,000 miles = 819,088,710 feet), forty million man days of effort would have been required to build them.[4] This is an awesome amount of manual labor by modern standards, but it is trivial when compared to the much larger effort of getting stones to the edges of the fields in the first place. That job usually had been done stone by stone, and load by load, by the previous generation.

Most of the time the stonework on a farm was just another mundane chore, no more exciting than chopping wood, flinging manure, or shoveling snow, and no more costly in terms of labor, since it could be done during slack times. Other statistics can also help put this seemingly Herculean task into its proper perspective. The United States population in the early nineteenth century was about 10 million souls. Assuming that only one person in three was young enough and strong enough to move stone, and that only one person in three lived in New England, each would have been responsible for building 248 feet of stone wall, scarcely a few weeks' worth of effort during a lifetime.

Data from the national 1871 Census of Fences indicate that the average length of stone wall around an average 107-acre New England farm could have been built with a two-man crew in less than two days per year. Two days out of three hundred sixty-five would have been devoted to clearing stone.[5] When compared with the equally mundane task of chopping and hauling wood, the average farmer probably spent twenty-two times as much effort to heat his home as to clear his fields of stone.[6] (Based on the amount of energy they used, I once calculated that a single college football team could wall in twenty farms per year.[7])

Converting the ragged wall into an acceptable one was done in conjunction with the final clearing of stones from a valued field. This often involved removing the largest glacial erratics, which had been left in place up to then. Farmers, with more time on their hands, and greater literacy, actually wrote about the challenge of moving big boulders. Some of them were blown up with explosives. Others were pushed sideways into deep excavations dug beside them, then covered by dirt. Inventive farmers created and patented fancy contraptions—rock lifters and grippers, slings from tripods, jointed levers—to wage war against those persistent big stones that blemished their otherwise flawless fields.

ာ

A FEW STONE WALLS WERE BUILT ABOVE WELL-DRAINED, FROST-free foundations. Here, the recommended procedure was to lay out a straight line, excavate a shallow trench to remove the fine-grained material that wicked water beneath the stones during freezing, and backfill it with gravel before skidding or rolling the basal stones into place. Usually, however, only the loose organic debris was stripped away. Then the actual stonework could begin.

When building walls, New England farmers used simple rules governed by the laws of mechanics, a branch of physics dealing with mass and motion. The field of mechanics includes both statics, the stability of materials at rest (which governs the shape of stone walls and the internal arrangement of its stones), and dynamics (the forces and movements associated with moving the stones). Both were equally important in the construction of stone walls, regardless of when or where.

With respect to "statics," the most important principle was to lay the stones down in horizontal tiers with their edges butted together. Each successive tier of stones was laid so that the gaps in one tier did not coincide with the gaps in the one above it. This principle, known as one-on-two and two-on-one, is perfectly expressed by brickwork. A second principle was to place the largest stones (especially if they were irregular) near the base of a wall where they could serve as a foundation for the smaller stones above them. Finally, walls were tapered upward, or "battered," to keep them from tipping over.[8]

The majority of a farmer's walls were little more than stacks of stones perched precariously upon one another. Closer to the house and barn, and nearly always around cemeteries, stone walls were usually built, from the start, with some care. Most often, they were built of both sides, forming a "double-faced wall." Whenever possible, the straightest and thickest edge of each stone was placed on the outside, and each was positioned so that it slanted inward toward the center of the wall. This technique helped make walls stronger with time because the stones pressed more tightly together as the wall settled. The center of each double wall, where the thin and irregular edges of both sides met, was usually filled with rubble and pebbles. As the walls were built upward from their boulder foundations, they were leveled off to create a roughly rectangular cross section, upon which a final tier of "capstones" was placed.

Capstones were slabs large enough to span both sides of a double-faced wall, heavy enough to press them together, and flat enough to be attractive; often they were culled from stone piles and reserved for the final tier, especially at gates and corners. Another specialty stone was called a thrufter. These elongated, almost spindle-shaped stones were placed inside a wall to help bind its two sides together. This was especially important at corners, where the stones from one wall could be overlapped with those of the other, like the logs of a log cabin or the dovetails in a wooden drawer. Sometimes, the stones were arranged in a decorative pattern—blocks and slabs, dark and slight, big and small—if the raw materials allowed it.

Stonework often is more carefully done near the end of a wall segment, regardless of whether it meets a corner or not; gaps between stones become fewer and smaller, the stones are chinked more tightly, the edges are aligned more carefully, and the top is laid flatter. Freestanding ends of wall segments are constructed as if they were "triple-walls," with the stones slanting in from both sides as well as in from the end. They are especially common at "bar-ways," places where primitive gates once stood before they rotted away. There, wooden rails called bars were raised or lowered and inserted into slots in the butt end of a wall to form a fence without the need for hinges. A stone stairway called a stile was sometimes built into a wall when a barway wasn't desired, but where pedestrian traf-fic warranted it. These were constructed most simply by letting the ends of a few strongly supported stones stick out from the wall.

The walls near barways and other primitive gates were built better, partly because there was a greater need for strength, but also for aesthetic reasons. It was here that the wall was seen most often by passing vehicles, flocks and herds of animals, and people—farmers, peddlers, children, evangelists, and strolling lovers.

Two segments merging at right angles form a corner. Many an imposing square corner quickly degraded to a pile of rubble with increasing distance. Solid corners were sometimes required after parcels of land had been resurveyed with the more precise surveying instruments available in the early nineteenth century—transits, theodolites, and levels. Conflicts over property boundaries needed permanent resolution, which often came in the form of a stone wall. Eventually, even well-defined wall corners would fall out of favor as more precise survey markers of iron pipes and concrete posts became the convention.[9]

Endless variations on these basic construction principles and techniques were woven into the stonework of Yankee villages. A doorsill required little more than a single large stone and something to prop it up with. At the other extreme were the walls around churchyard cemeteries, which often exhibit the most elaborate stonework, often capped with a top layer of quarried stone. A barn or outbuilding foundation required little more than a row of large slabs raised to the same elevation. The most evocative type of drystone wall is the house-size square surrounding old cellar holes. Stone cellars were built to support the basal timbers of a wooden house and to create an artificial cave below it, one that could be used to store food and that kept it cool in the summer and unfrozen in the winter.

In addition to stone walls and foundations, there were other, more unusual stone structures. Freestanding root cellars were built aboveground in the shape of igloos, a design that offered a tightly sealed chamber without the need for other materials. Stacks of stone set upon farmyard erratics sometimes rose upward into columnar structures as the stone kept coming, year after year. Short segments of walls occasionally begin and end for no apparent reason; they were most often upgraded piles of fence-line stone. Crescent-shaped segments of walls curved into the prevailing wind may have been sheep folds, where a huddled flock could wait out a passing storm. Isolated circles thirty to forty feet in diameter were stone-lined charcoal pits, where heaps of wood twenty feet high smoldered for days; their stones are usually oxidized to the brick-red color of fired pottery. Smaller circles with red-tinged, fire-cracked rock were the remains of campfires, which have been constructed on and off for millennia by Native Americans and by runaways and homeless travelers during the Yankee era. When such fire pits are densely concentrated, they are probably the remains of temporary encampments for war soldiers. Some stone structures were built for the sake of art, some for no discernible reason at all.

The American model of an upgraded wall was distinctly different from its British counterpart.[10] Many of the walls of western Britain are high enough to be legal fences, which is clearly not the case in New England, where most walls are thick and low. In Britain, they also usually have a top tier of stones—called copestones (not to be confused with capstones)—that are deliberately set on edge, like books on a shelf. This technique is extremely rare in the woodland walls of North America, and is typically present only in wealthy, old, thoroughly English communities like Newport, Rhode Island. Per unit weight, copestones exert greater stress on the flat-lying stones beneath them, bonding the underlying stones more firmly, making the top part of the wall more stable. They also provide painful footing for any animal jumping upon them, a function equivalent to iron spikes on top of a masonry wall. Finally, copestones look less natural, and less stable than when laid flat, sending a message of imminent collapse, one that might deter a recalcitrant sheep, filly, or calf from the prospect of jumping. Had stand-alone agricultural fencing been the paramount objective of stone walls in New England, many more would have approached the higher, more intimidating style of their Old World counterparts.

Nearly all of the walls in New England were built of unshaped fieldstone, stones simply picked up, moved from the field, then tossed or laid into a wall without mortar. In contrast, the walls in old villages or near houses and barnyards were often deliberately shaped, sometimes with little more than the whack of a hammer. Many stones still bear the marks of their shaping in the form of a lighter-colored patch where the stain, or patina, of the original stone was broken away. Chisels, wedges, and sledges were used for larger jobs such as splitting boulders to make capstones. Enormous blocks—especially those plucked from ledges for doorsills, capstones, and thrufters—usually required shaping with a primitive, handheld, spike-shaped, hammer-driven drill. After the right number of holes had been drilled to just the right depth in just the right orientation, a large slab could be broken, sometimes with fire, sometimes by hoisting and dropping it, sometimes with the blow of a heavy object. The telltale evidence of this type of quarrying can still be seen in the broken, cigar-diameter drill holes—called pin and feather marks—on the capstones of many ornamental walls. They are often spaced about ten inches apart.

Every slab of New England fieldstone contains a tiny remnant of the original tectonic stress imparted to it when the stone first became cool enough to behave as a brittle

Illustration of a Redding, Connecticut, farm.

solid. The direction of this force is from the inside of a stone to its outside, and is concentrated at right angles to foliation. This "inside-pushing-outside" force is the fatal flaw—the Achilles' heel—of all rocks. Exposed stones have no alternative but to break into smaller pieces, for there is nothing except the pressure of the atmosphere to push stones together. The glacier exploited this inside-to-outside force when it lifted the bedrock in large quarried blocks, and used this force to break the blocks apart. The weather exploits this force when it breaks large fieldstones in half as they rest quietly in the woods. Quarrymen exploited this force when they converted New England's rough ledges and boulders into tons of straight-edged building stone.

ᴄᴕ

WALKING IN THE WOODS OF NEW ENGLAND TODAY, ONE could get the erroneous impression that most of its fences were made of stone. Wooden fences, which were always more common than stone ones, simply vanished after the land was abandoned. This was true even during the early-nineteenth-century epoch of agricultural wealth, available labor, and Federalist optimism. The problem wasn't a limited supply of stone, for many areas had been deforested for nearly a century, giving plenty of time for stones to be concentrated by heaving and erosion. The problem was that a well-built stone wall was an expensive proposition, relative to a wooden fence, even then. We tend to underestimate the importance of wooden fencing in the nineteenth century simply because the wood has disappeared, whereas the stone has not. Wooden fence posts rotted at ground level, tipping their rails into the soil, where they were rapidly digested by soil microbes. Stone fences fall apart as well, but do so on a geological time scale rather than a biological one. Hence, they are still around.

The lithographs of John Warner Barber's "Connecticut Historical Collections" prove this point.[11] Seventy-four of his engravings "executed from drawings taken on the spot" show rural agricultural scenes typical of southern New England. Of these images, forty-five show solely wooden fencing, usually of the post-and-rail variety, and with the fourth rail as high as a horse's shoulder. Twenty-one of the scenes show some combination of stone and wood fencing, usually with one or more rails placed above the stone, and held in place by an A-frame of poles. Only 11 percent (8 out of 94) of his illustrations showed stone walls without wood, and these were always lower in height than wooden fences. As a fencing material, stone without wood was very rare.

More detailed data can be found in a document produced by the U.S. Commission of Agriculture in 1872, the first and last national census of fences.[12] At the time, fencing was an important factor in federal land-use policy, which was struggling to ameliorate disagreements, even bloodshed, between cattlemen, railroaders, and farmers over who bore the responsibility, and the privilege, of fencing the land. Essentially, the ranchers wanted the farmers to fence in their lands, whereas the farmers wanted the ranchers to fence in their cattle. This was a replay of the problem New Englanders had faced a century earlier during the transition from common herding to privatization of enclosure as the communal, Puritan style gave way to a distinctly American one. Questionnaires were sent to officially designated agricultural correspondents in every state and territory, 846 of whom responded. An anonymous statistician and author then compiled the report. It remains today as the best hard data on the phenomenon of stone walls at the time when they were most widespread, before many would be chewed up by rock crushers, buried to make way for larger fields, and poached for the suburbs of a subsequent century.

According to the census, the heights of fences in New England were typical of those elsewhere in the nation, ranging from three and a half to five feet. Stone fences were included in a category labeled "other," which included "worm, rail, cap-and-bunk, board, wire, hedge, log, brush, picket, and woven fence." The census also made it clear what nineteenth-century New England farmers meant when they said the word "wall" or "fence." To them,

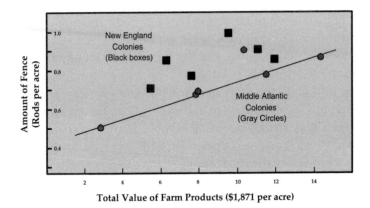

Amount of Fence (Rods per acre)

New England Colonies (Black boxes)

Middle Atlantic Colonies (Gray Circles)

Total Value of Farm Products ($1,871 per acre)

Graph based on data from the 1871 Census of Fences by the U.S. Dept. of Agriculture showing the strong correlation between farm productivity and the amount of fencing for the mid-Atlantic colonies (gray circles) and the New England states (black squares), where fences are more abundant and are unrelated to farm productivity.

a stone wall was any accumulation that reached a height of two and a half feet, regardless of whether it was part of a fence or not. A stone fence, in contrast, had to reach the legal height of four to four and a half feet without any help from rails. The hybrid fence—part stone on the bottom, part wood on the top—was very, very common. In Plymouth County, Massachusetts (an area the size of Rhode Island), fully 60 percent of the fences were "stone and wood combined," with only 10 percent as true stone fences. Thus, most stone walls were never legal fences, in and of themselves.

Within greater New England, the maximum concentration of stone walls varied widely. Rhode Island, with up to 78 percent of its fences being made (or partly made) of stone, had the greatest proportion of stone walls, followed by Massachusetts (60 percent), New Hampshire (51 percent), Connecticut (33 percent), Vermont (32 percent), and Maine (20 percent). The average price of a stone fence bore little, if any, relationship to either the price of wood or to the average population density on farms, which was related to availability of labor. These hard facts and statistical data refute the argument that stone walls were built primarily because labor finally became available, or because stone replaced wood when the latter was in short supply.

With respect to monetary value (the cost of stone versus wood), a stone fence made the most economic sense in New Hampshire, followed by Vermont, Maine, Rhode Island, Connecticut, and, finally, Massachusetts. Curiously, stone walls were most abundant where they were most expensive to build and rarest where they were least expensive. This is the opposite of what would be expected if material costs for fencing were the primary determinant. Something else was going on.

George Washington had spotted the problem. He may have been the first to recognize that "in the New England States . . . landed property is more divided than it is in the states south of them."[13] A comparison of twelve northeastern states, six in New England and six to the south (New York, Pennsylvania, Maryland, Virginia, Delaware, and New Jersey), showed that he was right; New England had far more "fences" than it needed, at least based on farm economics. Because fencing was usually the single biggest investment on a farm, often exceeding that of the land and buildings combined, the amount of fencing on any farm should correlate strongly with the combined value of stock and crops, even when the proportionately smaller sizes of New England fields are taken into account. This was certainly true in the states just south of New England; of these six states, only Pennsylvania, with its Dutch-German tradition of dense settlement, seemed off trend. In the six New England states, however, there was hardly any relationship between the amount of fencing and the value of farm products.[14]

The inevitable conclusion that must be drawn from this anomaly in the agricultural value of fences is that many of New England's so-called fences had little to do with agricultural production. The extra fences discovered by the 1872 census were, instead, walls built to hold stone. More than anything else, they were linear landfills, packed full of agricultural refuse that would not decompose. This claim is supported by an early-nineteenth-century analysis regarding the cost of constructing a fence made of stone in Farmington, Connecticut, relative to other types of fencing.[15] This study took into account the lifetime cost of erecting *and maintaining* a rod of fence for a period of fifty years.

ᴌᴏᴄᴊ

MANY STONE WALLS HAVE LASTED QUITE WELL, ESPECIALLY those that were actually built, rather than merely tossed; those that were placed on firm, dry soils; and those that have escaped the ravages of falling trees. They seem to have survived everything else that nature has dished out during the last two centuries: heaving soil, drenching rain, and dissolution. In his autobiography, a nineteenth-century farmer-mechanic-tradesman named Asa Sheldon gave specific instructions on how to build a good two-sided stone wall.

> *If you want to build your wall five feet high, and have it stand centuries, as I am sure you do, then make the base half the thickness of the height, and batter it on front at least one and one-half inch to the foot. Mind and never put so small stones on the top that a dog running over them will knock them off. If the soil be clay, take it out a few inches wider than the wall and fill in back with good gravel stones, otherwise the clay will run in among the stones, freeze, and heave them, and thus injure the wall.*[16]

Mr. Sheldon's recipe was effective because each procedure he used interfered with one or more of the physical mechanisms that bring down a wall. Gravel helps because it doesn't wick moisture downward to the frost line, and doesn't compact unevenly. Battering (narrowing the width of the wall upward) ensures that the center of gravity for the wall stays low, preventing collapse by toppling. The blunt, pyramidal shape in cross section distributes the weight evenly. Avoiding stones too small for a dog to kick down prevents a chain reaction of the kinetic energy associated with falling stones. Early-nineteenth-century wall builders knew their practical physics.

Mr. Sheldon's rules for wall construction are similar to the natural laws of the formation of mountains, which mimic the structure of carefully laid walls. The relationship between the strength of a mountain and its internal structure is especially clear in the high part of the central Appalachians, where the tallest mountains have the widest bases, and are also those where resistant strata have been slanted inward, toward the center of the highland from both sides, and those capped by a thick layer of hard rock.[17] This mountain form is identical to that of the properly built double wall, complete with capstone.

Many features of stone walls mimic nature, perhaps because stone walls, although constructed by humans, contain a large component of naturalness. The Native American author William Least Heat Moon experienced the hidden, persuasive force of nature as he passed through the northeastern United States, and recounts this in *Blue Highways*. There, while building a stone wall with a friend:

> ... *a strange things began to happen. We could feel an urging in the rocks, a behest to be put in just so, to be set where they would hold against the shifts of the earth, against the twists of the roots. They fit one way and not other ways. It was as if the stones were, as Indians believed, alive. The rocks were moving us.... We just followed the will of the wall, whatever came from the stones.*[18]

Choosing the right stone, structure, place, and height for a wall are partly subconscious actions that take place when humans allow themselves to be guided by natural laws, when they follow the "will of the wall."

Stone walls "willed" the farm fields of New England to be small because of the amount of energy required to remove stone to the edges of fields. Sam Deane, as early as 1792, advised against small fields because they interfered with cross-plowing and became seriously compacted by confined livestock. Yet, at the same time, he recommended small fields for what he called "disposing of the stones." The historian John Stilgoe was more specific.

> *Rock clearing explains in part the small size of colonial fields. Men understood the great effort required to clear fields larger than one or two acres, and slowly—especially in New England—they learned how much longer they spent clearing one eight-acre field than eight one-acre ones.*[19]

I have tested this simple idea quantitatively by writing simple computer models based on geometric considerations and by assuming reasonable distributions and concentrations of fieldstone, and reasonable dimensions for stone walls. Fields came in a variety of rectangular and triangular shapes, but most were made as square as possible. Assuming a square field in which rocks were hauled off by hand, one at a time, and assuming a hundred rocks per acre needing transport, clearing an eight-acre field of stone would require fifty-eight miles of walking, whereas eight one-acre fields would require less than twenty miles.

Subsequent computer models were used to investigate how other variables might have influenced the spacing of walls. A model called RimWidth calculated that the stone walls around enclosures smaller than two to four acres would waste too much space just to hold the stones on their edges. One called PlowTurn computed the time wasted in turning a plow and its draft horse around; for field sizes larger than two acres, the amount of wasted time diminishes rapidly. WallWalk computed the distance needed to transport the stone from fields of various sizes with, or without, a stone boat. Experimentation with these and several other theoretical models made it clear that the optimum trade-off between these conflicting needs was a square field between two and four acres in size.[20]

It is surprisingly difficult to determine the average actual size of New England's fields. Historic sources contain good data on farm size, and the proportion of improved and unimproved land, because this was an important issue for taxation. But the size of fields was too variable, too idiosyncratic, for good statistics to be kept. There is excellent data from Harvard Forest in Petersham, Massachusetts, where the pattern of stone walls was mapped accurately during the 1930s as part of a forestry disease research project attempting to understand how white pine blister rust spread from tree to tree. The walls had been mapped to create a base map for separate tree clusters.[21] A sampling was done of two hundred fields within an area of densely settled farmsteads. The median size of a field was two and a half acres; 80 percent were smaller than five acres; 30 percent were smaller than two.

The same calculus governing field size was solved intuitively by the farmer George Platt of Milford, Connecticut. A transcript of his comments to the 1872 annual meeting of the Connecticut Board of Agriculture survives.[22] Mr. Platt was so experienced with the concentration of stones in the soil that he deduced that the size of fields should be "about three acres," based on the number and spacing of the walls needed to hold the stone.

The geometric pattern of enclosures within enclosures, each rimmed in with stone, are also consistent with a partly natural origin. When settlement began, the fieldstones were more evenly distributed, at least statistically, as a consequence of the natural mechanisms that put most of the stones there. But over time, the initially more uniform distribution of stones became a segregated one in which stony edges (walls) surrounded stone-free centers (fields). If the walls around a field filled up with stone before the supply of fieldstone was exhausted, a good alternative for holding the excess stone was to create another wall, usually at right angles to the first, in order to maintain square fields. This subdivision process sometimes took place over and over, until the arrival of stones slowed down sufficiently. Thoreau mirthfully commented on this tight division of land by stone wall in his journals. "I am amused to see from my window here how busily man has divided and staked off his domain. God must smile at his puny [stone wall] fences running hither and thither everywhere over the land."[23]

The way walls grow around a field is also constrained by natural laws. For a square field, there must always be a band around the edge of every field where it makes sense to move the stones to the edge, rather than to any pile. Something similar happens when autumn leaves are raked from a yard bordered by woodland. I always start by scraping those leaves nearest the edge into the trees, then continue by making piles that I later haul to the nearest edge of the woods. Similarly, stones hauled from the zone nearest the edge of a field form an initial concentration around the perimeter, one that will increase with time as more stone is added. A load of stones from anywhere else in the field is a more complicated problem. As was the case with the piles of leaves, the shortest hauling distance between the load of stones and any fence line must be perpendicu-

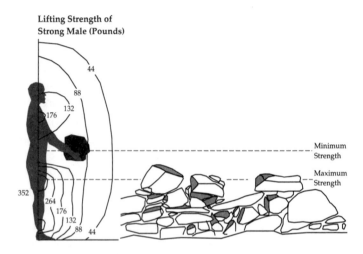

*Diagram showing a typical stone wall and why
it is thigh high.*

lar to the nearest edge. But the incentive to move stone in
that direction diminishes as one gets nearer the center of
the field. There, at the midpoint of a square field, all fences
are equidistant. At the midpoint of a rectangular field, the
two closest sides are equidistant. Corners will be the hardest places to get stone to, because they must always be farther away than any side.[24]

↳ଓ

Stone walls in New England are the height of a man's
thigh because of several ergonomic factors.[25] Lifting a
heavy stone to an overhead position—say, to the top of the
refrigerator—is not a smooth motion, but a series of three
discrete steps. Using the terminology of weight lifters,
there is the dead lift to the thighs, the curl to the chest, and

the overhead press to a straight-arm's length. Once the stone has been lifted, person and stone become a single mechanical entity with a common center of gravity. If the stone is held overhead, the spine can remain straight. Otherwise, the person must hug the stone in the front, against his stomach, or hold it sideways on the hip. This places considerable stress on the spine, which must bend either backward for a stomach-held stone, or sideways for a hip-held one.

In carrying a stone, the ideal position with respect to the vertebrae—straight above the head—is not only dangerous for the back but is the most wasteful in terms of lift energy. The lifting strength of the human skeleton reaches a maximum midway between the knees and the hips. This height corresponds to the thickest bone in our bodies, the femur—the height wheelbarrows are designed to be lifted, a stretcher is to be carried, and where handles are placed on large suitcases. At this height, a stone held at arm's length can be swung in a gentle upward arc like a simple pendulum hung from the shoulders. This gives the stone momentum in the direction of its arc, allowing it to move past the face of a knee-high wall. Before it descends to the top of the wall, however, the stone passes through a vertical position where it is momentarily weightless, allowing its final positioning to be achieved almost effortlessly.

Large, slabby stones can most easily be held by their ends, and can be swung efficiently only in front of the body. This means that they will be most efficiently tossed *across* the wall, an orientation that is also best for structural stability. Stones that are more chunk shaped have a greater concentration of mass and fewer convenient handholds; hence they are more easily pushed outward from waist height as they fall into place. Placing any large stone in a position higher than a person's hips is both difficult and dangerous. It was typically done only when the stonework was part of a construction project, rather than a fieldstone wall.

Slabs are the most convenient stones to clear and to stack. Moving a slab frees up more arable space than its round counterpart, and slabs are easier to lift because their edges make good handholds. They are also easier to carry because the stone can be held tightly against the body, bringing the combined center of mass closer to the legs that are transporting it, and therefore is more stable. But most important, the slab shape, like that of bricks or books, is easier to stack. Given all these incentives, it is no surprise that New England towns dominated by slab-shaped rocks are also those where the walls are the most common and the best built. The stone demanded it to be so.

ᴄᴏᴊ

IN THE EARLY YEARS OF THE NINETEENTH CENTURY, AN ERA OF optimism and improvements, the vast majority of Americans were still farmers, using their muscles and live-stock to create a human-dominated landscape. In New England, a small proportion of this energy was expended to create the beautiful stone walls now found throughout the region today. The placement of walls on the landscape coincides with nature's placement of the stones. The height, width, and simple structure of walls were deter-mined by the mechanical constraints of the human frame, whereas the quality of the walls was relative to the quality of the stone for building (slabs versus boulders). For areas of similar geology, the similarity in the physical form of the walls left behind by Yankee farmers—from Burlington, Vermont, to New Bedford, Massachusetts—is principally an expression of natural forces. Cultural forces also accounted for wall variation, but they were usually subdued beneath the economic mandate to move so much stone.

7

LAND ABANDONED

IRONICALLY, THE AGRICULTURAL IMPROVEMENTS OF the early decades of the nineteenth century set the stage for the decline that would gradually unfold over the next century. America's first utopia, the family farm, came to be seen less as a home to be lived in than as an exploitable resource to be managed for personal gain. This ideological shift coincided with the realization that the larger, stone-free fields of the prairies would yield a higher profit, given the transportation improvements that were taking place. Economic incentive rather than individual liberty and self-sufficiency became the guiding principle of land use. Survival was about finding the right market.

Technological changes helped drive the shift in land use. New England found itself in its most volatile epoch in terms of agricultural prices, which finally crashed during the panic of 1837. Unpredictable price swings, perhaps burned into the memories of individual farmers, had occurred during the previous two decades. Farming innovations, such as the cultivation of a new strain of melons, the invention of a new seed drill, or the development of a new pesticide, forced surges in the local market values for individual commodities. But more important, and more invisible, the volatility of New England farm prices was due to larger economic factors associated with the triangle of trade running from the Caribbean, northern Europe (especially England), and New England. The Louisiana Purchase (1803), the British trade embargo (1808), the War of 1812, the Panic of 1819, and the Panic of 1837 all had an impact on the standard of living for farmers, especially those in southern New England. Increasingly, farmers were held hostage to global events, one of which was the eruption of Tambora, whose volcanic ash darkened the skies, producing the Year Without a Summer (1816). Perhaps the solidity and security of a good stone wall provided some solace for farmers during these roller-coaster times.

The watershed decade for the decline of rural New England—with good times before and bad times afterward—took place between 1819 and 1829. It began with the market Panic of 1819—brought on by speculation and overextended credit—when the price for U.S. farm products fell to less than half their former, long-term average. This event was an alarm bell, signaling a transition from the old way of life to a new one, from a largely agricultural society to an industrial nation. In 1825, the completion of the Erie Canal was a pivotal event for many New England farmers, whether they realized it at the time or not. This celebrated opening of a new waterway heralded an era when durable agricultural products from upstate New York and the Great Lakes states began to pour eastward into New England, causing the price of commodities like beef and grain to plunge, and forcing many New England farmers to look elsewhere for a way of life.

The watershed decade ended with the construction of

the first overland railroad in 1829. The "iron horse" would, more than any other invention, revolutionize American agriculture. It set up a gigantic circulating current in which settlers were drawn westward by the prospect of new land, and their agricultural foodstuffs were drawn back eastward. "By the 1830s the notion that America was destined to absorb the whole of the West of the continent, as well as its core, was taking hold," according to the historian Paul Johnson. "This was a religious impulse as well as a nationalist and ideological one." Farmers who didn't ride the current to the West instead flowed downhill to the vigorously industrializing cities.

ᔭᑌ

PRICES FOR NEW ENGLAND AGRICULTURAL PRODUCTS MIGHT have risen again in the late 1830s and 1840s had it not been for permanent improvements in the transportation infrastructure, which also included substantial improvements to the road network and maritime port facilities. For-profit turnpike companies and overland stage companies worked together to greatly speed up surface transportation throughout the region. With few exceptions, the initial road network in upland New England had originally been laid out like a web whose strands extended from farm to farm, and which became concentrated only near town centers. Only after the advent of commercial farming, which required efficient, straight-line transportation to distant port cities and railroad yards, would substantial road improvements be warranted.

The mania for transportation improvements made possible the transition from oxcart to pleasure carriage. Boys and girls in farm villages now had an opportunity to see what urban life was really like. Once young people had had a taste of the larger world, it was more difficult to keep them "down on the farm." Rural life had been changed forever, and not necessarily for the better, at least in the mind of Farmington, Connecticut, resident John Treadwell, who later went on to become governor. He wrote presciently and emotionally of this cultural transformation in a report invited by the Connecticut Academy of Arts and Sciences.

> *That agriculture & commerce go hand in hand is true: but is equally true that farmers never flourish in a populous settlement where the commercial character predominates. The reasons are obvious—Commerce where it prevails creates riches, riches introduces a taste for luxury in building, dress, furniture, equipage & which agriculture can never support; the farmer is thrown into the shade. He feels that riches, as the world goes, gives preeminence. In homely dress & covered with sweat and dust, with weary steps returning from the field, he sees with pain the powdered beau rowling in his carriage with horses richly caparisoned, and feels himself degraded, his cheerfulness forsakes him; . . .This change is equally visible in the female part of our families; the young ladies are changing their spinning wheels for forte pianos, & forming their manner at the dancing school, rather than in the school of industry; of course the people are laying aside their plain apparel manufactured in their houses, & clothing themselves*

*with European & India fabrics; labour is
growing into disrepute; and the time when the
independent farmer, & reputable citizen could
whistle at the tail of his plough with as much
serenity as the cobler over his last, is fast
drawing to a close. The present time marks a
revolution of taste & of manners of immense
import to society but while others glory in
this as a great advance in refinement, we cannot help dropping a tear at the close of a
golden age of our ancestors; while, with a pen-
sive pleasure we reflect on the past & with
su[s]pence and apprehension anticipate the
future.*[1]

A decline in the population of oxen, once vital to New
England farming, was one of several barometers for changing rural conditions. Oxen were the tractors of their day,
slow but steady, and relatively easy to maintain. Yokes of
oxen hauled fieldstones in stone boats, hay in wagons, and
plows in the fields. And when they became too old and
tired they could be fattened up with pumpkins and corn,
then slaughtered for food. In 1850, there were 298,285
head of oxen in New England; within thirty years, their
population had fallen by more than 50 percent.[2] In an era
before tractors, fewer oxen meant that less heavy farm
work was being done each year. Part of the decline was
due to a switch from oxen to draft horses, which were increasingly being used to pull lighter, more modern steel
plows. But most of it signified a real job loss for this archetypal beast of burden.

The decline of the oxen population was mirrored by a

decline in the significance of stone walls on the landscape as farmers began to abandon the hill country in droves. This loss of population, already under way in some places for several decades, was punctuated by the American Civil War and its long aftermath of reconstruction. Surviving Union soldiers who left as hill-country farmers returned with a more somber, cosmopolitan worldview, one woven from the hardships of battle, the stories of frontier life, and the legendary gold rushes.

Before the Civil War, New England men made a choice: stay on their farms or leave. The default action was to stay. But after the Civil War, the same men had a different choice: stay away or return to the old way of life. This time, the default choice was to stay away. For many, the possibility of getting rich was too tempting to resist. For others, the gamble of losing the farm in uncertain economic times was too risky. The sheer boredom of farming drove others away. Although a few ex–New Englanders actually did find a pot of gold at the end of their personal rainbows (usually located near a factory, rather than a mine), most did not.

Other disincentives to remaining on hilltop farms included the Homestead Act of 1862, which gave away land rich enough to grow grass as tall as a man. Railroads began to reach fertile river valleys in California that were Edenlike when compared to the growing squalor of northeastern industrial cities. Worst of all was barbed wire, which came into widespread use after 1874. Before that time, fencing had been one of the most difficult and costly aspects of the farm effort. Wire fencing, however, made this job almost effortless, greatly reducing the cost of maintaining old fields and fencing in new ones. Inexpensive wire fencing thus raised the value of unfenced western land relative to those of the already fenced lands of the East, making it more alluring, acre for acre, dollar for dollar.[3]

The historians Elizabeth Forbes Morison and Elting E. Morison provide a specific example of this exodus from the hills and dales of New Hampshire.

> *As early as 1857, Professor J. S. W. Patterson had told the Grafton County Agricultural Society that in that very season 300,000 men and women had moved from the hillsides and valleys of New England to other parts of the country.... New Hampshire was not as good a place for farmers as it had once been. As soon as the rich soil of the Middle West was opened up, it could be seen that the rocky ground of the state had only marginal utility ... In 1840, half the ground within the state's boundaries had been cultivated land, but by 1870 only 39 percent was so designated, and in each remaining decade of the century this percentage was further reduced.[4]*

The population of upland farming communities plummeted, although there was no decline overall in the New England states. On a national level, the population shifted westward. "In 1790 [the] center of mass of the population was near Baltimore. By 1810 it was on the Potomac. In 1820 it was near Woodstock. By 1840 it was near Clarksburg in West Virginia, and by 1850 it was almost across the Ohio. In 1860 and again in 1870 it was still in Ohio, but in the decades 1880–1920 it slowly crossed Indiana."[5]

Although the economic downturn was pervasive in New England's rural hill country, it was the other way around for farms near cities where industries that had begun scarcely a half century earlier were intensifying and enlarging their workforces. Immigration from Europe accelerated throughout the nineteenth century; in the process, urban northeastern life was transformed from one of ethnic sameness to one with diverse customs and dietary practices. Aided by acceptable roads, strategic location, efficient production, and quick delivery to urban grocery stores and delicatessens, New England farmers near these expanding niche markets took up the challenge of feeding them all. Self-sufficiency had become an outmoded idea.

Agricultural productivity—rather than self-reliance—became the coin of the realm. New technologies helped farmers near cities stay in business. Ensilage, a process by which green fodder for dairy cattle could be maintained through the winter, was invented in 1876, and was to have a profound effect on the dairy industry. Silos, often attached to brand-new barns, sprouted like mushrooms where farms lay within reach of cities or dairy cooperatives. Chicken houses the size of factories appeared like magic in response to the demand for fresh eggs and poultry.

Another entirely new market for rural land also opened up: tourism. The perception of wilderness had changed from that of a hostile, unimproved place to one of sublime beauty. The Hudson River school of American painters—Thomas Cole, John Kensett, Alfred Bierstadt, George Inness, Frederic Church—translated this ideological shift into images. Resort hotels, now served by railway lines and improved roads, filled with guests retreating from the grimy, but lucrative, business of city life. Each hotel and tourist village was in need of fresh milk and eggs, forming dozens of small new markets for farmers close enough to reach them.

But most of upland New England lay too far distant from sustaining markets in the immediate vicinity of cities, mill towns, and tourist attractions. There, beginning with the remote hill country, on till-covered hills that were still excellent pastures, buildings went derelict and collapsed into their foundations. They disintegrated, leaving only, within the dirt, "small things forgotten," a phrase coined by the archaeologist Robert Deetz. Trees sprouted in old pastures like whiskers left uncut, enveloping their bordering stone walls in shade. Beginning about 1870, forest area began to double every twenty years or so.

As the trees came back, the walls came apart. Disorder was reclaiming order. The pioneering naturalist John Burroughs witnessed the moment.

> *One summer day, while I was walking along the country road on the farm where I was born, a section of the stone wall opposite me, and not more than three or four yards distant, suddenly fell down. Amid the general stillness and immobility about me the effect was quite startling ... It was the sudden summing up of half a century or more of atomic changes in the material of the wall. A grain or two of sand yielded to the pressure of long years, and gravity did the rest.*[6]

Walls collapsed downward, sending their stones rolling and tumbling inward, toward the fields and pastures from which they had come. Some stones must have fallen upon those in the act of being heaved up by frost, a process that declined in intensity as the mulch began to thicken again. The distinction between wall and nonwall became blurred as the boundary between civilization and wilderness faded, and as the land reverted to its pre-pioneering condition.

In Hanover, New Hampshire, I once watched a stone-mason quickly transform three sprawling piles of stone averaging thirteen feet in diameter into a segment of dry stone wall only two feet wide, fifty feet long, and two feet high. If spread out randomly on a flat surface, the stone in his tidy suburban wall would have taken up more space than the floor plan of the ranch-style house it decorated. This mason had done what thousands of anonymous New England laborers had done throughout the early years of the nineteenth century. By rebuilding a ragged fieldstone wall into a higher- "quality" one, they increased the "degree of order" within the wall or, more specifically, reduced its entropy.[7]

Investing order in a wall is the mechanical equivalent of winding a spring, or the chemical equivalent of recharging a battery. A spring, left to uncoil, must wind down. Batteries, left uncharged, must drain away. Stone walls, left untended, must fall apart. No matter the skill and effort of the mason, walls built up from stones in the soil and carefully arranged have no choice but to disintegrate and fall back to the ground.

A tray full of jumping beans—half red, half white—provides a useful analogy. Jumping beans "jump" because there is a worm writhing around inside them; the movement is intermittent, the direction random. When the active beans are unsorted, the top of the tray looks pink, at least from a distance. This pink world is a disordered system with low entropy; it can be compared to the "gray" world of light-colored fieldstones in a dark, cultivated field. Fieldstones move in the soil in response to frost heaving, tree growing, and animal burrowing; as with the phenomenon of jumping beans, the movement is intermittent, the direction random. The jumping beans will never automatically concentrate themselves on one side of the tray, or around its rim, provided that the system is left unattended and isolated from another source of energy. The same is true for the stones in the field; they will never automatically concentrate themselves into a rim or a wall.

But humans can intervene. They can cull the red beans to the sides of the tray, or cull the light-colored stones to the sides of the field. Both systems are now unstable from a thermodynamic point of view because they are more highly ordered, meaning they have less entropy. Left unattended, random motions ensure that the red rim of red beans will migrate inward, blending with the white ones, making the tray pink once again. A similar fate awaits the light-colored rim of stone around a field; it, too, will disperse back to the dark field.

When the farmer walked away from his stone wall for the last time, the human forces that caused the walls to be built up in the first place were replaced by the forces of nature, which will take them down. The forward part of this reversible ecological reaction—the construction of walls—was powered by solar energy, which was captured via photosynthesis in crops that were eaten and converted to mechanical energy in the stomachs of the farmers and their stock. The deconstruction of walls is also being powered by the sun. In this latter case, however, the solar energy is captured and converted to mechanical energy via wind storms, tree roots, animal burrowing, chemical disintegration, running water, and seasonal frost. Given enough time, and if left alone, the stones that were once concentrated in the form of the wall must eventually be dispersed back to the field. There, they will be further dispersed into the volume of the soil, buried once again by soil processes, making it appear as if the land had never been cleared.

ဟဝ

SEVERAL INVENTIONS ACCELERATED THE DISAPPEARANCE OF walls from the countryside, especially where walls were convenient to the road network. The rock crusher, invented in 1852 but improved and made portable only in the late nineteenth century, was a stone-eating monster. Fieldstone that was formerly waste now became a resource that would feed the seemingly insatiable demand for crushed stone, now vital for surfacing roads encumbered with traffic between farm and city.

Increased demand for fieldstone also came from the cities, where stone was still preferred over concrete for constructing bridge abutments, culverts, wharves, and seawalls. A farmer could sell his stone fence, replace it with a brand-new wire one, and, in the process, make a profit. Stone, once an encumbrance, had become an export crop. Ironically, some of the earliest stone walls originally built from quarried stone would, two centuries later, become quarries for building materials.

The transition to large-scale mechanized farming did further damage to stone walls. Faster, horse-drawn implements such as harrows, drills, manure spreaders, and multi-bottomed plows required fields that were larger, flatter, and better drained. Draft horses, which replaced oxen as the primary source of muscle power, were used to help take down walls built up a century earlier with yokes of oxen hauling stone boats. To make fields level, some walls were dismantled and spread into low spots at the corners of fields, then veneered with enough soil for tillage. To make fields larger, walls were knocked down and carted away. To improve drainage, stone was pushed into ditches that were back-filled to form underground drains.

Walls in the woods that were hard to get at or too massive to move were left standing as they were. Within decades trees grew nearby, protecting the walls from vehicle access. Unusually beautiful walls or those that still marked legal property boundaries were usually left in place, and they, too, were soon surrounded by forest.

Just because the farmer and his livestock walked away did not mean that the stone-generating processes ceased to operate. On many farms, the stone kept arriving via erosion and frost heave, cobbling and roughening the land surface, and making it nearly impassable, in some places, for wheeled vehicles. Even when preserved, however, walls everywhere were tumbling down, losers in their battle against nature.

ဟ

STONE WALLS, ALTHOUGH SUSCEPTIBLE TO QUIET EROSION, are surprisingly strong. In 1755, New England experienced its largest historic earthquake, which occurred near Cape Anne, Massachusetts.[8] Although most of the houses remained intact, their chimneys were thrown down, church bells rang, dishes clattered in cupboards, and, in certain places, the earth gushed muddy springs. The earthquake was felt as far away as New York City. In Connecticut, more than a hundred miles from the epicenter, the flow of water to wells was permanently changed, perhaps because blocks of bedrock shifted about.

The quake was violent enough to rattle down a few tottering stones near the top of stone walls and to lurch the ground back and forth between the agitated stones. A printed broadside read:

> *The birds flew flutt'ring through the Air,*
> *The Cows and Oxen lowed;*
> *And the Stone-fence the country round*
> *Lies scatt'red O'er the Road.*[9]

Although the earthquake caused the failure of some walls that were about to fall down anyway, it was, based on a reconstruction of ground-wave amplitude, nowhere nearly strong enough to throw down to the ground well-built, carefully laid walls. No earthquake since then has tipped so many stones.

Earthquakes aside, the key to the forces that bring down stone walls in New England is not their power, but their patience and steadiness. Over the centuries, stone walls have come apart grain by grain. The chemical breakdown of walls begins as soon as their stones are exposed to the elements. As rain soaks a wall, the chemical bonds holding crystals together are disrupted atomically, producing salts, oxides, and clay minerals that, as they expand, help pry apart the grains. Having come "unglued" from the rock matrix, the grains, each a chemically liberated crystal, are now free to be dislodged.

Sometimes, this process can actually be heard, especially on sunny spring mornings after a cold night if one's ear is placed at the gap between several stones. A gentle, irregular noise, something like low-frequency static or the crackling of an ice cube, is the sound of the rocks expanding in response to the morning's heat. Punctuating the static will be a louder (but still tiny) snap, followed by a tiny sprinkling noise; this is the sound of a single grain detaching and falling somewhere within the wall.

It is this grain-by-grain chemical weathering that gives stone its rough surface texture. Before weathering, the original surfaces of joints are quite smooth. But over time, an irregular surface develops. Resistant grains and veins of quartz become bumps and ridges, whereas chemically weak grains such as mica become hollows. This is especially evident on glacial erratics, which have been exposed to the elements for more than ten millennia. Their surfaces are much rougher than those of fieldstones, which, although weathered to some degree, have been exposed for a few centuries at most. Still, every stone exposed at the surface, including those in walls, is like a statue in the process of being sculpted; what remains is that which hasn't been dissolved away by time.

Chemical weathering is intensified at the points where two stones touch each other because water clings longer there, especially in the shaded recesses of a wall's interior. This increases the dissolving effect of weathering during summer and the shattering effect of ice in winter. Touching points are also the places where the weight of the wall is most concentrated. This concentration of physical stress adds to the concentration of weathering to ensure that those stones pressed most tightly together by gravity will crumble and crush the fastest.

The loss of a sand grain from a touching point leads to diminished mechanical support and shifts the stone's center of gravity slightly. Both effects invisibly alter the balance of forces in the wall. Eventually, the out-of-balance stone must shift, usually causing it to settle slightly. Sometimes, however, the shifting of stones near the base of the wall may cause the entire thing to tip over. This is probably what John Burroughs meant when he wrote, "A grain or two of sand yielded to the pressure of long years, and gravity did the rest." The changing balance of forces ensures that walls are never at rest. They just look that way.

Mortar, or cement, does little to hold walls together in New England because the lime of the concrete and the slight acidity of most fieldstone abhor each other chemically. Acids leached from the leaves of trees do greater damage. Even when well bonded, mortar makes the wall rigid, unable to flex with the strain of the swelling, shrinking, and stretching that take place constantly within the soil. To this extent, the classic unmortared fieldstone wall acts like a flexible stone chain; the mortared wall acts like a rigid bar with thousands of weak places.

ᴗᴄᴊ

SEVERAL MECHANICAL PROCESSES, FUELED BY THE RADIANT heat of the sun, break down stone walls one stone or one patch at a time. Consider the opening lines of one of America's best-loved poems, "Mending Wall," by Robert Frost.

> *Something there is that doesn't love a wall,*
> *That sends the frozen-ground-swell under it,*
> *And spills the upper boulders in the sun;*
> *And makes gaps even two can pass abreast.*[10]

Robert Frost

The "something" that knocked down America's most famous stone wall was not one of the "elves" invoked later in the poem, nor a passing hunter or deer. Instead it was a chain of events set in motion by the flow of heat energy.

The upward heaving of the soil by frost each winter, and its subsidence each spring, plays an important role in breaking down walls. Frost heave, the same lifting process responsible for raising stones from the soil, also lifts walls. Unlike stones, the lifting is usually unequal. One side of a wall may rise more than the other side, causing it to tip. Alternately, one section of a wall can rise like a blister beneath the skin, setting the stage for collapse.

Stones are especially restless in late winter—during sugar maple season—when the soil is cold, snow lies upon the ground, and the sun's warmth increases every day. The darker color of stone and a wall's elevated position cause it to absorb much more of the sun's heat than the snow-covered soil. This heat is conducted downward to melt the frozen soil and snow. Meanwhile, the weight of the wall has compacted the soil, reducing the size of the pore spaces between its soil particles and enhancing the soil's ability to transmit water by capillary action—wicking it from south to north, from warm and wet toward cold and dry.

Given enough time, ice accumulates beneath the northern side of the wall, pushing or heaving its stones upward. Meanwhile, the southern side of the wall has experienced little to no uplift. The difference in uplift between the north and the south sides of the wall cannot be compensated for by shifting within the wall itself, because the stones at the base of walls are typically large. Instead, the large basal stones translate the differential uplift into a rotational motion that tips the wall toward the south, as though a wedge were being driven beneath one side of a bookcase. As the tipping proceeds, stones start to slide or roll out of position. Finally, they fall in a chain reaction, a noisy cascade of stones falling to the south.

Even the best-built drystone wall will eventually fail in places where the soil wasn't right, where the original stacking was flawed, or where a supporting stone disintegrated too quickly. The damage from shifting stones or collapse is always local, because it cannot propagate down the length of the wall in a domino effect.

∽

THE TREES OF THE FOREST ARE THE ALL-TIME CHAMPIONS AT ruining walls, even more so than frost heaving. Sometimes this happens violently, when their trunks and branches crash downward. Trees caught in the act of dying do great damage to walls. The distance between tree and wall controls the kind and extent of collateral damage that occurs when a tree falls down. A tree falling from a great distance away strikes the wall like the flat side of a soft broom, whisking a few stones from a large area in all directions. A tree rooted closer to the wall will strike a hard, hammerlike blow with its trunk, crushing some stones and scattering many more in an outward direction. A tree rooted against the base of the wall makes the deepest gap because the full momentum of the moving tree—tons of pressure per square foot—is levered sideways against the wall's base rather than downward on its top. Each tree in the forest has a "sphere of influence," whose center lies at the base of its trunk and whose radius is governed by the height of its crown. Any wall within that territory is in danger.

Damage also occurs when the seedlings sprout in the rotting debris on top of a wall, especially in the center of double walls. Most seedlings die young, but sometimes they manage to send their roots down to the soil through the center of the wall and grow to considerable size. When these trees fall, they can lift up the entire section of wall within their network of roots.

Most tree damage occurs gradually, from growing trees. Tree seeds sprout and survive better in the darker, shadowed recesses next to stone walls or among their fallen stones because of the extra moisture, warmth, and wind protection. Also, chipmunks and squirrels cache their seeds among the stones, which then germinate inside the wall like an extremely slow time bomb. Or a young tree growing nearby sends its roots under the wall, where the compacted soil provides better structural support; as its roots get bigger, the mature tree can dislodge the wall's basal stones, tipping the entire stack of stone.

Walls often have gaps that resemble broken teeth in an otherwise perfect smile, each gap having been knocked out by a single tree. Intense damage to a wall can take place during hurricanes, which blow down dozens of trees in the same direction. Sometimes there is an interesting asymmetry to the pattern of fallen walls. East-trending walls more often collapse to the south, in response to stronger heaving of their northern stones. Walls on slopes fall downhill. Walls in areas where hurricanes strike regularly tend to be knocked to the north and northwest, the direction that blown-down trees tend to fall, which is generally away from the coast. Walls surrounding cleared pastures are always pushed inward, because it is only outside the clearing that trees are permitted to grow.

When a wall has no gaps, a stone can only fall forward or backward. But once a gap has been created, stones on either side of the gap have an opportunity to fall sideways, too. Thus, each gap accelerates the failures to come because it removes the structural support for the remaining stones. In this self-reinforcing process, walls can quickly become low and tumbled, with only a few "peaks" remaining to mark the original height. A corollary of this process is the stability offered by a low, broad wall, which will stay that shape for nearly forever.

∽

THERE IS A QUIETER, LESS DRAMATIC BUT MORE INSIDIOUS killer of walls that takes place on slopes. The soil, creeping under the influence of gravity, actually pushes them around as it flows to every low spot in the landscape.

Invisible because it moves too slowly, the upper foot or two of the soil literally flows downhill as a sheet, something like frosting on a cake that's too warm. Evidence of this process can be seen on forest trees, because the soil of deeply rooted trees is often thicker on the uphill side, where it accumulates; conversely, the soil is thinner in the downslope "wake" of the tree. Smaller, more shallowly rooted trees that were tipped by the process can right themselves, and, in the recovery phase, develop a permanent "elbow" where the trunk meets the soil.

The effects of soil creep are easy to recognize in the vicinity of stone walls. A wall built across the slope interrupts the flowing soil, causing a buildup on the uphill side. If the wall is strong enough, its uphill side will fill completely with soil, creating a drier, sod-covered terrace that looks just like a retaining wall purposely built into the side of the slope. Usually, however, the pressure of creeping soil exceeds the strength of the wall, pushing it over. If the remaining portion of the wall is strong enough, the soil will flow through the gap, taking the fallen stones along for the ride.

Soil creep—the steady, grain-by-grain movement of particles beneath the litter—is a ubiquitous phenomenon within New England soils. Constantly at work are the simple processes of wetting and drying, heaving and thawing, root growth and dieback, and animal activities. For example, a particle carried to the top of an anthill on level land will roll randomly outward in any direction, forming a symmetrical cone. On a slope, however, a greater number of particles will roll downhill, producing an elliptical pile much larger on the downhill side. Something similar happens when frost heaves a pebble, or when a tree—its roots full of dirt—falls over. Always, there is a net transport of soil grains downhill. Soil creep ensures that streams never run out of sediment. It is from such creep-filled hollows near the springtime water table that small ephemeral tributaries get their granular debris and send it to rivers, which, in turn, drain to the sea to make beaches.

Soil creep is responsible for pushing cellar holes inward. Originally, the weight of the wooden superstructure of the house was enough to keep the stones in place, and close to vertical, so the creeping soil could move past the foundation. However, when the house was gone, the inward horizontal pressure of the creeping earth was able to push the stones into the cellar, one tier at a time, from the top down. Many collapsed cellars now look like leafy sinkholes, their stone walls hidden like buried treasure below the mulch and brush.

ᔕᕮ

REGARDLESS OF HOW THEY GOT THERE, AND IN WHAT STATE of preservation they are, stone walls are now an important part of the ecological fabric of New England. They are not an alien rocky intrusion into otherwise pristine woodland; natural stone ledges have always been present, especially during the first few thousand years after glacier recession. Besides, the concept of pristine woodland is in error. The forests have always been changing in response to climatic, biological, and cultural events. What was most different about the European agricultural conversion of the New England forest was not that one type of tree was replaced by another—for example, chestnut by white pine—but that the organic soil on which the forests depended was changed.

The modern flora and fauna of the forest respond daily

to the grid of stone walls on the landscape. The collective influence of walls, especially where they are dense, may actually exceed the influence of other agents like fire, erosion, or selective logging.[11] When the land was in agricultural production, stone walls were barriers between different types of land use, perhaps corn on one side, hay on the other. Those walls set the stage for a cascade of biological events still under way. Even after the initial colonization of abandoned farmland by trees, walls became firebreaks and stream banks, seedbeds and watersheds, ridges and terraces, all separating elements in the landscape. Old walls are also physical edges between growing places. In this regard, many low walls make better fences for woodland flora than they ever did for cattle, which could step over most of them. The Northeast's secondary forest is a grid of quirky patches, each carrying with it the legacy of past land use. In other words, there is a historical component to the vegetation on either side of every wall.

But walls are also habitats, independent of the contingencies of history. They are places without soil, hard, rocky places in an otherwise soft habitat—barrier to some creatures, but homes and highways for many more. Rattlesnakes once basked on the sun-warmed stones. Now it is their prey that dwell there, baby woodchucks beneath the stones and chipmunks between them. Foxes, raccoons, feral cats, and children use walls as roads to cruise their territories. At various times, walls are refuges where animals hide from predators, blinds to ambush prey, and places to build a nest or to live in obscurity. Stone walls, especially tumbled ones, incubate nuts—acorns, hickory, walnut, beech, chestnut—and the naked seeds of conifers—hemlock, pine, spruce, fir, tamarack. Walls are corridors for animal life, allowing migrations that would otherwise have been impossible.

Stone walls also control local microclimates. Northern sides are always darker and colder than their southern counterparts. East-facing sides are warm in the morning and cool in the afternoon, with the opposite being true for west-facing walls. Walls also influence the length of shadows, the intensity of the wind, and the persistence of snow in complicated ways.

Each wall is also a climatic buffer because it can hold a large quantity of heat and release it slowly; to this extent, a gap near the base of the wall acts as a shallow cave whose temperature varies less than that of the outside air. The wall is also a much better conductor of heat than the soil flanking it because it lacks the insulating quality of the forest mulch. This means that the soil surrounding the wall remains warmer in the early winter and colder in the spring than near the center of a stone enclosure. Stone is cool to the touch on blazing-hot days, and warm at night, something that a toad might notice. If moss and lichens are the common companions of walls, it is, at least in part, because the dew collects on walls and stays there longer than in most other places.

All of these effects, accrued since the time of farm abandonment, have transformed a complicated woodland ecosystem into an even more complex one, one capable of sustaining more biodiversity. If New England has more lizards and snakes and stone-dwelling insects than it once did, it is because its walls are the closest habitat we have to the rocky, desiccated slopes of canyons.

∾

STONE WALLS HAVE AN ACTIVE ROLE IN THE MOVEMENTS OF water within watersheds. For example, walls built across small floodplains can stop the flow of sediment-laden floodwaters, converting a forested swamp to a natural meadow. If buried completely by alluvial mud, such walls can act as natural drains beneath the floodplain. If blocked, the water percolating through the stones can seep upward like an artesian spring. Stones thrown in streams long ago, for any purpose—to make a ford for cattle, to slow the effluent from a millpond, to protect a bank—usually lie near where they were first tossed, often forming a small cascade in the modern stream and improving trout habitat in the process.

Under normal forested conditions, even the heaviest rainfall is not intense enough to cause surface runoff. Instead, it seeps into the ground, then moves downhill—above the impermeable hardpan, but below the ground surface—through large pores such as roots, burrows, and fractures, finally emerging just above streams. When these pores are compacted beneath a wall, however, subsurface seepage can erupt just uphill from the wall. A gathering rivulet, unable to move the stones, instead cuts downward into the soil on the uphill side of the wall, creating a small stream that will enlarge downhill until it is deep enough to flow during subsequent storms. The wall has given birth to a stream.

Walls can, more rarely, influence coastal wetlands. Based on long-term tide-gauge measurements, the sea level is rising along most of the New England coast at a rate of several millimeters per year, due largely to the melting of small glaciers, thermal expansion of the oceans, and groundwater withdrawals. Some of the earliest walls were

built on small marshes below till-cloaked coastal promon-
tories, which provided the boulders. Now, during high
tide, they are stony islands and peninsulas, gathering
grounds for shorebirds.

Rising sea level has increased the rate of bluff erosion,
which now threatens a few coastal lighthouses. Some
stone walls on such clifftops have already fallen seaward,
one stone at a time. If enough of the bluff has eroded, and
if the stones are big enough, the line of the fallen wall
might be preserved on the beach, like a miniature pier
now smothered by sand on the berm.

ᴄᴆ

Gone are the nineteenth- and early-twentieth-century
farmers. Their cleared fields are crowded with tree
saplings, competing with each other within an evolving
forest ecosystem. Former wooden buildings have surrendered to gravity, fallen to the soil, and been consumed as
nutrients recycled back into nature. Even lost iron tools
have rusted out of sight.

Many of the stone walls of that agricultural era have
since been foraged as quarries for raw stone or have been
buried. Although the remainder have been weathered,
leached, heaved, tipped, buried, hammered upon by trees,
and eroded by coastal storms, they persist, even if in a ruined condition. They still exert a profound influence on
the living landscape by being habitats, corridors, and
edges of habitats. In this regard, it is probably not fair to
consider the land as having been abandoned at all.

8

RURAL REVIVAL

IMPROVEMENTS IN TRANSPORTATION—THE CON-struction of canals, railroads, turnpikes—were an important factor in the decline of New England's rural economy in the late nineteenth century. Radically different improvement in transportation during the early twentieth century reversed that decline. The gasoline-powered "horseless buggy" would, almost single-handedly, repopulate rural New England, a trend that continues unabated today.[1]

The first Ford Model T cars rolled off the assembly line in 1908, and became affordable to the middle class within a decade. More than 15 million had been sold before the line was discontinued in 1927. The pneumatic tire, invented in 1916, increased the speed at which New Englanders could move along their bumpy roads. Leaded gasoline gave them the power to climb any hill and the distance to reach nearly everywhere. No longer were the vast majority of New England urban dwellers tied to the thriving metropolitan areas where they lived. Easier to keep than a horse and carriage, the automobile provided city families with the freedom to reclaim New England. Some were close enough to commute.

By the turn of the twentieth century, Governor Frank W. Rollins of New Hampshire was distributing a promotional document titled "New Hampshire Farms for Summer Homes." President Theodore Roosevelt held a "Country Life Commission" in 1908 with the stated goal of enhancing the quality of country life. Cities that were once magnets for country folk reversed their polarity, sending many residents to the country, especially on weekends. Other inventions made rural life even more attractive, notably electricity, refrigeration, and telephones. Americans of the Gilded Age, the Jazz Age, and the Roaring Twenties, their economic success assured by industrial achievement, went looking for their roots on the farm. For the first time in American history, the compelling story of rural life was not agriculture, it was tourism and respite. Wild lands were no longer places to be feared: They were a tonic for the anxiety of urban life.

Other rural activities contributed to the revitalization of rural New England. Chief among these was forestry, which reinvented itself as a business and a profession as the trees grew back and when pulp paper was invented. Timber companies went on a splurge, buying trackless land. Universities, notably Harvard and Yale, responded by creating schools of forestry, which have since evolved into schools of environmental science. White pine—the weed of former pastures—became a commercially important wood product used to make boxes and cartons in an era before plastic and fiberboard. Tree farms, something an eighteenth-century pioneer would have had trouble conceiving of, sprouted up in abandoned fields. Planted in straight rows like corn, but taking longer to reach harvestable size, trees were planted as crop monocultures.

Maple sugar began to flourish as an export business now that the sugar maples, having sprouted in old fields and woodlots, had become good sized. The forestry salvage operation following the great hurricane of 1938, which blew down a swath of trees between Long Island, New York, and northern Vermont, brought thousands of underemployed city dwellers to the forested interior, many of whom never returned to the city.

Conservation, as a discipline and a profession, appeared outside the timber industry; wildlife, soil, and water were its principal themes. With urban America becoming increasingly dependent on public water supplies, trained scientists began to see watersheds as integrated natural systems rather than as geographic areas; hydrology, which evolved as a discipline within engineering, became an outdoor profession practiced by many other disciplines. Clean water and flood hazards became hot topics as early as the turn of the century. Between the Great Depression of the 1930s and the Cold War of the 1950s, engineers responded by building flood-control reservoirs, dams, and floodways on all the major rivers in New England, in an act of ecological hegemony that has since never been matched. Meanwhile, scientifically minded conservationists set the stage for the professional "environmental manager" who would appear scarcely a half century later, and for whom clean water, rather than wildlife or soil, was the defining management objective.

Farming, especially large-scale dairy operations, adapted as well and remained successful. Pasteurization and homogenization of milk, refrigeration, and sterilization of bottles allowed the milkman to become a familiar sight. "Milk sheds" expanded until they coalesced across the region. Specialty farms—the tobacco industry along the Connecticut River, apple orchards throughout Massachusetts, potatoes in Aroostook County, Maine, and poultry "ranching"—survived by increasing the scale of their production while simultaneously narrowing their markets.

და

WITH THE REDISCOVERY OF RURAL NEW ENGLAND DURING the early twentieth century, the technical professions focusing on the outdoors began to take more notice of stone walls on the landscape. Archaeologists, landscape architects, physical geographers, foresters, soil scientists, and engineers began to locate and describe them, often incidentally. Yet never in these objective disciplines did the subject of stone walls flourish. It was in the subjective domain of the humanities—art and literature—that stone walls would soon become hallowed ground. In a process that began slowly, beginning with the end of the nineteenth century and continuing up to the middle of the twentieth century, stone walls were being filtered through poetry, paintings, novels, photographs, and oral traditions, to become more potent visual symbols than sugar maples and church steeples. Eventually stone walls would become the signature of the New England interior landscape. As the writer Howard Mansfield states, we put them back *In the Memory House.*[2]

The changes in attitudes toward New England stone walls is illustrated by how artists, especially painters, treated them over the years. Works of the Hudson River school, painted before wholesale abandonment of hillside New England in the mid- to late nineteenth century, focused on the sublimity of nature, emphasizing the wild and primitive, rather than the tame, and the spiritual conquest of what was once wilderness.[3] Their paintings of the northeastern United States contain hardly a fieldstone except for those shown in natural clefts and chasms.

In contrast, painters of the Impressionist school during the early twentieth century couldn't paint enough fieldstones. The art historian Harold Spencer writes:

> *The images created by these painters have a familiar look . . . [and] reveal the native sources of these Impressionistic images ... old farms weathered by the years, fields mottled by outcroppings of ledge and sectioned by the ubiquitous stone walls ...*[4]

Many of these painters gathered along the Connecticut shore, in places like Darien, Fairfield, Old Saybrook, Old Lyme, and New London, close enough to New York but away from the city's hustle. At the abandoned property bought by the Impressionist painter J. Alden Weir and converted into a summer artist colony, they were able to paint an unusual mix of wall styles and forms; many of those paintings hang in galleries today. Some stone walls they painted were so primitive that they are little more than elongated piles. They also painted tossed walls from the time when the farm was cleared and pastured, and ornamental walls that conveyed a sense of wealth and protected privacy.

Weir, apparently not satisfied to paint landscapes, laid his own stone walls or hired masons to do the job in his stead. In one place, he framed a stream in stone, channeling it into a hidden rock gutter to ensure that it would stay where he wanted it. In another, he broke up a continuous wall, then marked its ends with colossal stones that look like pillars. If a wall interfered with his artistic vision, like the one on the ledge above his private pond, it was deliberately pushed over, tumbling back into its constituent fieldstone fragments.[5]

As the century rolled along, Currier and Ives manufactured thousands of images of rural New England, often painted with snow and sleighs in the foreground, and farmhouses and playful children in the background. The artists made sure to put fieldstone in nearly every scene, even if it was no more than a solitary boulder beneath a wooden fence. Stone seemed to be an essential ingredient for their art.

Photography would eventually overtake landscape painting as a way to portray the essence of rural New England. Samuel Chamberlain, the "photographer-laureate" of New England, used stone walls to grace his masterwork, *The New England Image*. Photographer Wallace Nutting[6] sold thousands of hand-tinted pictures of stately maples and blossoming orchards in his effort to romanticize, even sanitize, New England's past. Fanatical to show urban dwellers what they were missing, Nutting published his photographs in six volumes, titled *Beautiful Maine, Beautiful New Hampshire, Beautiful Vermont* . . . , each arranged by county. Altogether, 293 of his photographs showed rural agricultural scenery. Nutting's photos provide an extraordinary archive on the subject of stone walls, revealing that rural scenery was seldom complete without these ancient, decorative piles of refuse stone, now properly tainted by time.[7]

Old stone walls, deliberately left out of earlier paintings, were now being painted into scenes, whether they existed in the actual landscape or not.

Ironically, the reduction in the physical visibility of stone walls between the mid-nineteenth century and the mid-twentieth century—by collapse and decay from natural causes, by their stones being stolen, and by the reforestation of the pastures they bounded—steadily increased their cultural visibility. A convincing explanation for this delayed reverence for what was once commonplace comes from a short, somewhat obscure, but seminal work by J. B. Jackson. He said historical preservation

> ... *sees history not as a continuity but as a dramatic discontinuity, a kind of cosmic drama. First there is that golden age, the time of harmonious beginnings. Then ensues a period when the old days are forgotten and the golden age falls into neglect. Finally comes a time when we rediscover and seek to restore the world around us to something like its former beauty. But there has to be that interval of neglect, there has to be discontinuity; it is religiously and artistically essential. That is what I mean when I refer to the necessity for ruins ... the old order has to die before there can be a born-again landscape.*[8]

The "old order" of rural New England died slowly during the latter half of the nineteenth century, when the population from upland farming towns became intoxicated by the industrial power of cities and lured by the promise of the West. Conservative talk about the nobility of agriculture did little to stop the exodus of Yankee youth. New England had entered its interval of neglect. Pastures became woodlands, buildings collapsed, and machinery dissolved into rust. But the stone walls of that lost civilization survived as the remains of fences, cellar holes, graveyards, barn foundations, animal pens, charcoal pits, sheep folds, fords across streams, collapsed milldams, and odd piles. Carried forward with the stone were the oral traditions of a romanticized past.

The "new order" accelerated dramatically in the early twentieth century with the realization that America—first as an idea, then as a nation—had been conceived of and defended by independent English farm families living in small rural towns where individualism mattered. In art and architecture, this ideological shift became known as Colonial Revival, a backward-looking, somewhat sanitized view of the way things were, or the way certain groups thought things should have been. This cultural transition was fueled, in part, by those who were well off imagining themselves returning to a golden age, an epoch when cities were not overcrowded with European immigrants and with American blacks migrating northward from the Jim Crow south. U.S. immigration had already passed its peak near the turn of the century, and the nation was now adjusting to its consequences, most of which played themselves out in American ghettos.

Looking upstream from thriving industrial cities, those with opportunity acted on their "necessity for ruins" by seeking out artifacts of the golden age such as saws, axes, sap buckets, chisels, guns, sledges. They also reconstructed early villages to an idealized form, devoid of the poverty and squalor of the authentic past. Most important, they re-

Henry David Thoreau

furbished stone walls on rural properties that had been abandoned only one or two generations earlier.

These stone walls evoked in their new owners a feeling of a deep, almost mystical connection to America's past, especially when stumbled upon in the deep woods, where they are encrusted by lichens, stained by dissolving leaves, toppled by heaving soil, and smashed by falling trees that have long since rotted away. Instinctively, even casual observers could sense the human presence within each wall, knowing that each of its stones had once been lifted by a living, breathing person. By touching a stone, one could almost touch the hand of the anonymous person who had placed it there and appreciate the simple integrity of that life.

The very soul of New England had somehow gotten mixed up with rural farmstead walls. Henry David Thoreau penned his reverence for them in an undated journal entry for the year 1850: "We are never prepared to believe that our ancestors lifted large stones or built thick walls . . . How can their work be so visible and permanent and themselves so transient? When I see a stone which it must have taken many yoke of oxen to move, lying in a bank wall . . . I am curiously surprised, because it suggests an energy and force of which we have no memorials."

Robert Frost, poet laureate of New England and the sage of stone-wall worship, gave much thought to the "energy and force" pondered by Thoreau. His books are brimming with boulders and hardscrabble lives. More than any other person, Frost is responsible for weaving stone walls into the American consciousness. For him, stone walls were more than symbols. They were oracles.

> *Some may know what they seek in school*
> *and church,*
> *And why they seek it there; for what I search*
> *I must go measuring stone walls, perch on*
> *perch;*[9]

Frost went beyond using derelict stone walls as powerful memorial symbols. He elevated them to the stature of the supernatural. "Pan with Us" begins with these lines:

> *Pan came out of the woods one day—*
> *His skin and his hair and his eyes were gray,*
> *The gray of the moss of walls were they*
> *And stood in the sun and looked his fill*
> *At wooded valley and wooded hill.*[10]

The eyes of Pan—playful Greek god of the forest—are the gray stones in New England's walls. Robert Frost understood that the "valley and wooded hill" had to be abandoned and reforested before Pan could come "out of the woods one day." He understood, as J. B. Jackson would later explain, that ruins require a period of separation, a period of neglect, a time for the walls to tarnish with time. Later, the writer Eric Sloane rendered the walls into the memorials sought by Thoreau. "The plain farmer of two hundred years ago was weaving the fabric of a new nation and although there are no marble statues to his patriotism now, there are still his stone walls."[11]

Through these and other writers, New England had learned to love its stone walls more as memorials to a lost world than they had ever been loved as fences. A psychological curtain had been lifted, revealing what had been there all along.

ᴸᴼ

THERE'S MORE TO THE AESTHETIC ALLURE OF STONE WALLS than their memorial associations. Each is a work of art in and of itself. Every wall reflects personal—in some cases, artistic—choices made by its builder, from the selection of location to the size, shape, and placement of each stone.

Stone walls are aesthetically pleasing to all the senses. Sometimes stone walls even make music when two stones are struck. Each yields a different pitch and tone: clunk, thud, clatter, ping, rattle, and tap. The wind brings softer sounds to stone walls exposed on the edges of cleared fields and roads. Each catches the wind like a sail full of holes, compressing it through rigid slits, each a different size and offering a different edge to the wind. When the wind is blowing strongly, especially in winter, you can hear various pitches, depending on gaps between the stones and the velocity of the wind blowing through them.

The texture of stone walls can also be enjoyed using touch. Most stones are grainy and rough, with uneven surfaces and irregular lumps. But some stones are gracefully curved, others as flat as a tile. Some are polished smoothly, like a bowling ball; others are jagged and pointy, even dangerous. Some are colder and warmer than others. When wet with dew or green algae, some feel slippery.

As visual objects, stone walls have form, color, texture, shading, perspective, and endless variety. Their geometry varies from sharp-edge, angular slabs to perfectly rounded boulders. Their shading varies from the dark tones caused by deep shadow and heavy patina to the sun-bleached tones of the highest stones. Some walls have a grain like wood; others are a hodgepodge of form.

Color is perhaps the richest visual experience of stone walls. The pallet, although usually gray, ranges from rust to black. Mineral colors on exposed stone surfaces are usually dusky, or slightly powdery, owing to corrosion and the bleaching done by the rain and the sun. On a wall, the color of a stone is a blend of its constituent minerals. Muted earth tones become more vivid on freshly broken fragments, or when the stone is soaking wet. This effect is exaggerated even more when a stone is sheathed in ice because the ice refracts light like a lens. After an episode of freezing rain, green, lavender, and pink are intensified in a wall.

Quartz is a light-gray, often greasy-looking mineral common in coarse-grained stones. Mica crystals grow in the form of flexible sheets whose surfaces sparkle like shiny plastic. Feldspars are off-white in color and always break along gemlike facets. Calcite, one of the earth's most common minerals, is usually missing because it dissolves too easily. Dark minerals—pyroxene, olivine, graphite, hornblende, tourmaline, magnetite—are abundant in the volcanic rocks of the rift valley. Accessory minerals have more unusual shapes—soccer-ball-shaped garnets, crosses of staurolite, and cubes of pyrite. They embellish stones all over the Northeast. Children, who prospect stone by instinct, frequently mistake muscovite for gold and quartz for diamonds; their treasure hunting usually ends when they realize that something so beautiful can be worthless.

Life brings color to a wall in ways other than its minerals. Lichens paint the stones with pastel greens and brownish grays, although some are bright yellow, others reddish. Lichens are primitive plants (actually symbiotic masses of algae and fungi) that manufacture acidic solvents capable of dissolving the stone, allowing them to attach firmly, as though glued by epoxy. Lichens are very sensitive to the availability of sunlight, being as dense as chain mail where the light is strong and as sparse as polka dots when in complete shade. Another primitive plant, moss, remains green, even when frozen. Mosses are common where a wall is moist and shaded. Deciduous leaves and coniferous needles also decorate walls with brown colors, except in autumn, when the hues are more vivid. The deadfall from branches, especially when being consumed by slime molds, bracket fungi, mushrooms, and other decomposers, bring to walls almost every conceivable living color, from bright purples to iridescent oranges.

Walls in the woods can also change the olfactory landscape of their immediate surroundings. Most stones don't have much of an odor. If you smash or grind a small stone into dust, there is only a faint, earthy smell. It is life in general and microbial decay in particular that gives smell to the northeastern woodlands. Volatile elements such as carbon and nitrogen and sulfur are captured from the atmosphere by growing plants, used to make organic matter, then released again during decomposition in the forest mulch. When stone walls are warmer than the soil around them, they enhance local odors. When colder, walls are freer of the fragrance of soil. During a heavy rain, especially in late fall when the leaves are pressed flat to the ground, stone walls become vents for the aromatic gases being expelled from the soil by the infiltration of water, somewhat like a row of smokestacks above a microbial refinery that's fermenting away underground.

We even taste our walls. Unless artificially distilled, all of earth's water, including urban tap water, carries with it the dissolved constituents of stones. Marble is dissolved most easily, followed by brownstone, slate, schist, and gneiss, then granite. Sodium is most easily lost, followed by calcium, and potassium, and magnesium, at decreasing rates. If not absorbed onto fine soil particles, or drawn into roots of plants, this dilute stone soup seeps down to the water table, where it flows slowly but surely to streams, wetlands, and wells. Thus, we imbibe our stones, our walls, recycled in every glass of water we drink, whether in bottles or from the tap. Earth's water, even in the snows of north Greenland, is mineral water. Our bones and teeth are built from it. Walt Whitman celebrated this concept in the opening lines of "Song of Myself:"

> *I celebrate myself, and sing myself,*
> *And what I assume you shall assume,*
> *For every atom belonging to me as good be*
>   *longs to you.*[12]

The stock market crash of 1929 and the ensuing Depression combined as a death blow to many of the farms that remained. Thousands of New England farmers went belly-up. Many of their properties went into receivership for back taxes, then were transferred to the public domain as state parks and forests, thousands of which grace the countryside today. Other farming communities became water-management areas, like Quabbin Reservoir, which supplies water to Boston. Its impoundment flooded an entire nineteenth-century farming village, preserving it for posterity like a sunken shipwreck. With less money for leisure, many grand resort hotels fell into disrepair. With the population of tourists gone, the farmers who once fed them had no choice but to leave as well. For at least a few years, in some rural places, New England seemed to have been abandoned, once again, at least physically. But the allure of stone walls was there to stay.

9

‍‍

BACK TO NATURE

ONVENTIONAL NEW ENGLAND AGRICULTURE IS
now in its death throes. Dairy farms survive only
with price supports. Sheep are being slaughtered as a precaution against hoof-and-mouth disease. Poultry farming has gone south, where facilities can
be heated more cheaply. The last tobacco farms in the
Connecticut River Valley are under assault by real estate
developers who are razing their disintegrating barns to
make room for gated communities and condominiums,
by environmental bureaucracies who are suing them for
past pesticide pollution, and by neighborhood activists
who are offended that tobacco is being grown near their
homes.

So tough are things for farmers that legislatures in
every state have passed laws to preserve the farming way
of life as though it were an artifact from an earlier age, preserved for the sake of preservation. Each week there are
articles in local newspapers throughout New England an-
nouncing that some farm family, perhaps ten generations
in the making, has sold the development rights for its
property to the state, or to a nonprofit trust, in exchange
for the right to live there in perpetuity.

Conventional agriculture may be dying, but farming is not yet quite dead. In fact, it's beginning to thrive again. Specialty farms are cropping up everywhere, selling anything that needs soil or space to grow. Near cities, organic and communal vegetable farms thrive, producing hormone-free milk, antibiotic-free meat and free-range poultry, and specialty ethnic vegetables. Some of the most successful new farms have gone underwater, raising salmon, oysters, and, recently, a whitefish called tilapia. New England farmers sell acres of sod, ornamental shrubbery, flowers, specialty seeds, and bulbs to greenhouses and garden stores. Whatever grows is being sold in progressively narrower, wealthier niche markets. This is an economic pattern opposite to that of late-colonial and early Yankee farmers, who were initially nearly self-sufficient, exporting almost nothing.

Of all the trends and inventions of the last half century, however, two stand out as having a lasting impact on rural New England in general, and on stone walls in particular. Most important was suburbanization, also known as sprawl, made possible by the interstate highway system of the 1960s. Safer, more comfortable cars and cheap gasoline contributed to the problem as well; they made long-distance commuting not only possible, but practical, thereby driving up energy demand and its consequent pollution. Several other factors raised the demand for buildable space in the suburbs, which has sometimes been described as America's second utopia[1]: upper- and middle-class flight from the inner cities; the housing needs of baby boomers and their families; and the large increase in the retirement population with disposable income augmented by Social Security.

The era of high technology is contributing to sprawl in different ways. Unlike other traditional industries, the information-processing industry did not need to be headquartered near rivers, railroads, canals, or the sea because nothing except electrons was being transported. Since the most important resource was a steady supply of electricity, software firms and dot-coms simply moved to where their generally well-educated employees were already living, the outer edges of suburbia. This spawned yet another surge in the demand for housing, even farther out, one that has produced a "halo" around the older suburbs. Many workers telecommuted, going to the office weekly or biweekly.

Abandoned farms in almost every New England town are now being divided into housing lots and sold to real estate developers. Ironically, the minimum size for many rural lots in New England is two acres, nearly that of a tightly enclosed stone field. This small size is determined by the need for on-site sewage disposal via septic tanks and drain fields, so as not to damage wetlands.

The distinction between suburbia and truly rural areas is fading into something called "ruburbia," being neither suburban nor rural but a blend of both. Sprawl has inaugurated a second round of significant deforestation, this time to make room for housing developments, shopping malls, schools, and golf courses. Moving outward from cities on all sides, ruburbia has now consumed much of rural New England, nearly everything within a one-hour drive of any medium-size city.

Nowhere is this more evident than around Boston, which has three concentric interstate highways surrounding it: I-93, I-95, and I-495. The Connecticut River Valley—

once a rift zone, later a glacial lake, then the breadbasket of New England—is also nearly fully developed, from New Haven at its southern end, to Brattleboro, Vermont, at its northern.

The environmental movement of the late twentieth century was the second dramatic change to affect stone walls, both positively and negatively. During the earliest years of the movement, which spanned the late 1960s and 1970s, much of the focus was either on toxic waste or on preserving wilderness areas. As the movement matured, the focus shifted from wilderness protectionism and acute problems with "good guy–bad guy" scenarios to more long-term issues emphasizing the ethical treatment of animals, quality of life, and sustainability. The movement also shifted consumers toward so-called natural materials. It was the merger of "quality-of-life" issues and "natural" materials that stimulated the second rediscovery of New England's stone walls.

Answering the call of the early conservationist Aldo Leopold, whose *Sand County Almanac* spoke eloquently about land being reclaimed by nature, and Rachel Carson, whose *The Sea Around Us* asked us to pay more attention to what we take for granted, New Englanders began to seek out and occupy derelict farms. Many young families and retired individuals were drawn to the country not so much for its pleasantness but for the integrity of life possible there. Unlike the repopulation of rural backcountry in the age of the Model T, this movement was precipitated less by a desire for a respite from the world than by a desire to reform the world, at least locally.

Unfortunately, there has been a dark side to the back-to-the-land movement. Many large-scale ruburban devel-

An old woodland wall in a forest.

opments, especially those larger than five acres, have captured in their curved web of cul-de-sac property lines part
of the square web of the historic stone walls that were on
the landscape when the property was bought on speculation. When left intact, these old stone walls, like outdoor
antiques, helped grace their properties. Most suburban
lots, however, lack stone walls, a desirable and almost indispensable part of modern rural architecture. To build the
walls, stone must be hauled onto these lots, and is often
"borrowed" from other walls—either on the property, or,
more likely, from somewhere else.

Throughout New England, gravel-pit operators, land-
scape-supply businesses, and excavation companies now
buy whatever old walls they can find on speculation, then
sell them to masons who are willing to pay top dollar. Old
stone walls are being disassembled, tossed into trucks,
transported across state lines, and rebuilt as ornaments.

Older stones are highly prized. Those whose surfaces have been darkened by a century of corrosive rainfall, whose muted colors are blotched by lichens, and whose cracks are filled with organic material—leaves, twigs, colonies of moss, animal nests—are deemed more beautiful, more natural than freshly quarried stone, which, in New England, is almost metallic in its appearance because of the abundance of mica. Ironically, those people still living closest to the land—farmers struggling financially to hold on—have a strong incentive to sell their walls. Old stones, which only a century earlier were considered refuse, are now valuable raw material. Stones have become a cash crop, but they can be harvested only once. Farmers have every right to sell stone, just as the new owners of the stone have every right to buy it and use it in whatever way they want to. But individual property rights need not *always* supersede the right of a region to enjoy its common history, contained within its stone walls.

With the price of fieldstone rising toward $500 per ton, and with environmental regulations on quarrying fresh stone becoming more restrictive—because it requires blasting and alters drainage—the destruction of woodland fieldstone walls will continue to accelerate until it is finally recognized as the environmental tragedy it is. Like termite damage, this ongoing process is largely invisible because it happens away from scenic roadsides and parks where walls are protected by local, state, and federal ordinances. It will stop only if society makes it financially and culturally worthwhile for the owners of old farms and new houses to leave existing walls intact.

The loss of an old wall is particularly heartrending when it is a cellar hole, the primitive, stone-lined basement of a dilapidated, abandoned house. Already gone are the noises of children and the fragrance of wood smoke. Long ago fallen to the oblivion of the soil are the square nails, lost buttons, broken glass, and all else. With the cellar hole cannibalized and its hole backfilled, there is nothing left to mark the home's past except for the rim of brush surrounding the old cavities: red sumac, wild rose, blackberry, and mountain laurel, whose roots seek the moisture of old dirt floors. Such cellar holes, or "dents in the earth," as Thoreau dubbed them, should be left in peace. Each is the grave of a house.

Taking walls apart to build new ones is akin to disassembling a fine piece of antique furniture and using the wood to make a new piece. On a community scale, it is the equivalent of taking down a crumbling historic lighthouse to build a modern, efficient one with the same material; something is lost in the process.

There is more at stake here than a few walls on a few old farms. Ecological diversity is firmly established within the network of abandoned walls. Stone walls are the dryland complement to the wetland habitat so vigilantly protected by local, state, and federal laws. Archetypal fieldstone walls, especially tumbledown, nondescript, even ugly ones, deserve greater protection as well, whether through market, legal, or ethical mechanisms.

Luckily, many stone walls already have legal protection because they occur in parks, other public land, or along designated "scenic roads" and historic districts. Others are protected simply because landowners value their charm and integrity. The vast majority of stone walls, however, are privately owned, and survive simply because the demand for stone has yet to outstrip the supply. Every

day more fieldstone walls are harvested from abandoned
farms as though they were trees being logged from a
forest. The trees can grow back. The stones cannot, at
least not until the next ice age, which doesn't do us much
good.

Moving walls from one place to another homogenizes
the rock landscape in an unsettling way. Geologists in New
England have always used the stone in walls as a clue to
what lies beneath, for there is usually a close association.
For them, brownstone intuitively *belongs* in one place,
marble, schist, and granite in others. To find a wall made of
schist standing in terrain underlain by marble is like seeing
a brick ranch house in the midst of an old colonial district
of clapboard houses. This is, for most people, an aesthetic
concern. For geologists, it is an ethical one.

ဆ

ALDO LEOPOLD'S "LAND ETHIC," WHICH EXTENDED ETHICAL
considerations to the land on which we live, helped stim-
ulate late-twentieth-century reoccupation of rural New
England. His concern was with the duality between man
and nature, a struggle with deep historic roots in New
England. The eighteenth-century observer Hector St. John
De Crèvecoeur wrote of America's pioneering mind-set:
"Thus, one species of evil is balanced by another; thus the
fury of one element is repressed by the power of the
other. In the midst of this great, this astonishing equipoise
Man struggles and lives."[2] The historian Perry Miller
claimed that the struggle of nature versus civilization is
not *an* American theme, but *the* American theme. This
struggle, however, particularly as it applies to the wilderness, is paradoxical. Henry David Thoreau noted that "it is

vain to dream of a wildness distant from ourselves."[3] More than a century later, the historian William Cronon extended this line of thought:

> *This, then, is the central paradox: wilderness embodies a dualistic vision in which the human is entirely outside the natural. If we allow ourselves to believe that nature, to be true, must also be wild, then our very presence in nature represents its fall. The place where we are is the place where nature is not ...We thereby leave ourselves little hope of discovering what an ethical, sustainable, honorable human place in nature might actually look like.*[4]

Pulitzer Prize–winning scientist Edward O. Wilson ascribes dualism to contrasting human self-images.

> *[The] naturalist self-image, which holds that we are confined to a razor-thin biosphere within which a thousand imaginable hells are possible but only one paradise. What we idealize in nature and seek to re-create is the peculiar physical and biotic environment that cradled the human species ... The competing self-image—which also happens to be the guiding theme of Western Civilization—is the exemptionalist view. In this conception, our species exists apart from the natural world and holds dominion over it.*[5]

The distortions of dualism are timeless and global. *Man and Nature,* published in 1864 by George Perkins Marsh, has been appropriately labeled the fountainhead of the conservation movement. Marsh saw man as ". . . everywhere a disturbing agent." He was the first American author to systematically assess the unanticipated environmental consequences of deforestation on a global scale, although there is no record that he made the connection between deforestation and the transformations in the soil that led to the thousands of stone walls surrounding his Vermont village. More than a century later, Bill McKibben's *The End of Nature* presents a similar thesis regarding the dichotomy between man and nature, but with a focus on newer problems like greenhouse warming and stratospheric ozone depletion. Whether we have *ended* nature or not depends entirely on whether we consider ourselves part of it or not.

ഗര

STONE WALLS, VIEWED WITHIN THE CONTEXT OF HUMAN ecology, can help clarify and smooth out the rough edges of the relationship between man and nature. Since its inception in the 1930s, ecology has become a well-developed scientific discipline that increasingly pays heed to the role of humans in all things. Clearly, stone walls were built by human hands, yet the building was accomplished within an "agro-ecosystem" within which both social and biological constraints were important.[6] From this environmental history point of view, stone walls should not be considered victory monuments in a war against nature, as Curtis Fields claimed in his 1971 book *The Forgotten Art of Building a Stone Wall:* "In these walls

George Perkins Marsh

there is solidity and strength and an imperviousness to Nature's force."[7] Nothing could be further from the truth: Stone walls are perpetually being weakened or destroyed as a result of freezing and thawing temperatures, fallen trees, water damage, and so on.

Within the context of human ecology, stone walls can now be seen primarily as landforms, assembled by human hands, but designed primarily by the constraints of nature. They were made by people who possessed enough metabolic energy to move stone out of their pastures, but not enough to haul it any farther than the edge of the field. Stone walls are clearly genuine *artifacts*—meaning they are physical objects that were deliberately fashioned by humans and that say something significant about the human past. They are also biological *ecofacts*—something built at least in part by nature.

Noel Perrin, in his essay "Forever Virgin: The American

An ant hill.

View of America," defined nature broadly: "So what I'm going to call nature is everything on this planet that is at least
partially under the control of some other will than ours."
Nature is that "other will."[8] Nature, then, is the entity responsible for producing much of what we see in many a
New England wall. The ecofact component.

ᴸᴏᴄᴖ

AS A CHILD, I SPENT COUNTLESS HOURS WATCHING THE COM-
ings and goings of ants in sandy, vacant lots. They went to
war against invaders, biting each other into bits and pieces.
They assembled teams to carry off enormous meals: dried-
up worms or pieces of cookie, freely given for the sake of
experiment. But above all, I marveled at the uniform shape
and spacing of their mounds, or anthills. I wondered how

the ants could create such perfectly symmetrical shapes. Why do the mounds so closely resemble miniature volcanoes, especially cinder cones?

The answer is that ants don't care about the shape of their hills any more than a volcano cares about its cinders. Anthills occur because ants dig out chambers hidden below the ground surface, the place where they live complicated social lives—taking their meals, feeding the queen, and raising their young. The anthill is a sort of dump site for sand or dirt, merely an outward manifestation that is quite incidental to the ant's task of living an underground life. Any beauty to be found in the shapes of anthills and cinder cones must be credited to the physics that govern the flow of granular material away from a central orifice, whether one speck of sand or one piece of pumice at a time. On both anthills and cinder cones, the larger grains roll farther because they have more momentum and are less well packed. This leads to gentler distal slopes than those nearer the central orifice, which, in turn, leads to the parabolic shape.

In the vacant lots of my childhood, anthills caught my attention. In the woodlands of my adult life, stone walls do. A century ago, before fields were abandoned and trees reclaimed the land, there was an active farm—perhaps with an orchard, a field full of pumpkins, or a herd of woolly sheep. At that time, the focus of the farmer's attention would have been on what mattered most—the arable field with its sweet-smelling soil, the source of his livelihood. When faced with needing to clear a pasture or plant a field, the farmer probably carried the stone refuse to the edge of the field, whether by hand or by sled. There, he tossed or set it upon the other stones that had accumulated along the fence line, probably working with no more ceremony than the ant dropping its grain of sand on a slowly growing hill. Neither ant nor farmer thought about the beauty of what he was doing. The mind of the ant is too small. The mind of the farmer was probably too preoccupied with what mattered most: the fate of his children, the smell of his breakfast, the mood of his wife, his unspoken dreams.

In a sense, the wall nearly built itself, very much like the hill of the ants builds itself. It grew, almost automatically, something like a linear crystal growing stone by stone instead of atom by atom.[9] To grow, crystals need little more than atoms and chemical energy. To grow, stone walls need a pastoral economy, stony ground, a place for disposing the stone, and an affinity for straight lines. The form of a wall is determined by the size and packing of its constituent stones. It is for this reason that fieldstone walls look so similar, regardless of which continent they occur on, or which culture built them.

From the perspective of the geologist, the most important role humans played in the story of New England's stone walls was not the actual tossing of the stones one upon the other to make walls. Rather, it was the catalytic effect of humans deforesting the land and exposing the soil. This removed the climatic buffer of the forest and the protection of the organic mulch. It also steepened the energy gradient between air and soil, precipitating a series of changes that caused stones to concentrate at the surface. After this catalytic phase, the farmer participated in the ecological reaction—to clear his fields, he piled stones at field borders, then concentrated even more stones into tossed walls. The final act of abandoning the fields was almost as important to the story of stone walls as the initial act of clearing the forest. Without abandonment, the walls would have continued to function as expedient fences and boundary markers, keeping them within the domain of vernacular architecture. But by walking away, each farmer bequeathed to the woodland ecosystem a new type of landform—the tumbling down wall—one that would, two centuries later, assert its influence on the terrain throughout New England.

Like the ant, the New England farmer disposed of the waste without giving it much thought. Directing the stones to fall in a certain place as they were being tossed required a trivial amount of extra effort that came at the end of a long sequence of events—finding, lifting, carrying, loading, off-loading, carrying, and tossing. Tossing the stones into a border, rather than tossing them in an amorphous heap, paid off handsomely in terms of disposing of waste stone, while simultaneously creating a fence and establishing an aesthetically pleasing form. Conversely, the care and attention required to build an intensely ordered or carefully chinked drystone wall was almost never practiced around fields and pastures. Nature's economy is manifest in the classic, slightly ordered pasture wall.

10

WRIT IN STONE

THE MODERN ERA IS A TIME OF EXAGGERATED urgency and detachment from things natural. Our food is genetically modified, our clothing comes from synthetic fabrics, and our electricity is produced by nuclear reactors. Our daily routines are increasingly overwhelmed by electronic devices—cell phones, beepers, faxes, Palm Pilots, wireless transmitters, Internet streaming, etc. Information flows so quickly that television has become interactive. Unfortunately, the distinction between real and unreal, between authentic and virtual, is fading away, especially for children.

Part of us yearns for contact with something simple and honest, like homespun cloth. Fieldstone walls, especially old, decrepit ones, give us that simplicity as well, being so elemental in form and function. They are also unambiguous evidence of a Yankee culture that expired midway through American history. This makes them almost as sad as they are simple.

Stone walls were once as mundane as they were ubiquitous. Like trees in pastures, and small brooks, they were noticed but given little thought. Farmers' journals and account books, as well as published eighteenth- and nineteenth-century farming manuals and magazines, seldom contain more than a sentence or two about the subject. With rare exceptions, no more attention was given to stone walling than to shaving or hanging the laundry, as it was little more than a routine farm chore.

Today we are able to appreciate stone walls perhaps because "we no longer *have* to build them," as noted by Kevin Gardner, writer and master builder of stone walls. Instructions on how to build stone walls can even be found on the Internet. Stone masonry has become much more than a respectable trade; for many it has become a well-paid craft. Gordon Hayward, horticultural writer and stone-garden designer, documents the increasingly urgent desire for stone as a landscaping material.

> *Twenty years ago, when I started designing gardens here in the Northeast, stone supplies were limited to very few choices....Now I visit those same yards, and others across the country, and see rows and rows of cut bluestone, sandstone, and limestone for patios and pathways. Piles of inexpensive granite cobble and lichen-covered boulders on pallets are ready to go, as are rounded river rocks, granite fenceposts to mark garden entrances, cast-stone pavers, stepping stones, cut stone benches and garden ornaments, or palletized wall stone from all over the country ... All this, and stone walls going up everywhere.*[1]

It's hard to explain why stones have become so popular. Kevin Gardner, author of *The Granite Kiss* (which takes its title from the slight wound, the scraped or gently smashed finger caught between stones during the process of wall building), says stone walls convey an "almost primal impression of order and safety." This may be the case for those who are contemplative by nature or artistically minded or interested in historical preservation.

But the appeal of stone walls is much broader. They have become the icon for the hero-farmer, one whose legacy is made of fieldstone. Gradually evolved through colonial and Yankee oral traditions, this was no ordinary man. With a rifle in one hand and an ax in the other, and standing stoically between his glistening plow and patient team of oxen, he conquered the wilderness, did battle with the stones, won, and then vanished. Susan Allport's *Sermons in Stone* elegantly describes the relationship between the hero-farmer and stone walls. "Written in these walls are eloquent reminders of the odds against which the early farmers of this area worked, tilling thinly soiled ground whose main claim to fecundity was the abundant crop of rock that heaved to the surface each winter."[2]

Like all myths, there is a grain of truth in the construction of the hardscrabble hero-farmer. But there are several distortions, which, once revealed, give way to a more universal means of celebrating walls.

ဢ

EASIEST TO DISPENSE WITH IS THE MYTH THAT FARMING IN general and stone walling in particular was a male activity in which brute strength and tenacity were the most celebrated values. It wasn't. Patience was the predominant virtue. New England's early farmers were a patient and pious *group* of people—man, woman, girl, and boy. They created America by working:

> *Hand to the Plough*
> *Wife to the Cow*
> *Boy to the Mow*
> *Maid to the Sow*[3]

The role of women in New England farm activities was summarized by Elizabeth Forbes Morison and Elting E. Morison, authors of *New Hampshire:A Bicentennial History:*

> *Insofar as liberation is a function of equality, the women were liberated: they worked just as hard as the men—and somewhat longer. The average membership in the family in the first part of the last century was 6.7, and mothers did most of the things necessary to feed and clothe that membership. They often tended the garden; invariably processed, one way or another, all the foodstuffs; often picked and cleaned the wool; usually spun and wove and cut and sewed. They washed, scrubbed, mended, fed the young stock, raked scatterings in the haying season, administered herbal teas to the feverish, picked apples in the fall, bore 4.7 children and—especially in the first two decades—brought in a good deal of the family cash.*[4]

The walls and farm tools remain as testaments to the heavy muscular work, done generally by men. Comparable testaments to the work of women are disproportionately small, because most of their effort was spent working with organic materials, few of which have survived, except in the form of progeny. More important, in retrospect, the stoniness of New England has been exaggerated. Agricultural reports make it clear that New England soils in every state were, during the seventeenth and eighteenth centuries, and remain today, highly fertile when managed wisely.[5] Stone was an annoyance throughout the region, part of the bargain a farmer made when he wished to have good hillside pasture, which, in turn, meant glacial till. And even though clearing of this stone was a large effort, it was dwarfed by the much, much larger effort of running the farm, most of which left no trace of physical evidence.

The hero-farmer of New England is the Eastern counterpart of the cowboy of the American West. Cowboy, horse, and pistol merge into a symbol for western settlement, and for the rebirth of a nation after the Civil War. The eastern version is the farmer-citizen Thomas Jefferson had in mind when he helped frame the U.S. Constitution—the man with a three-cornered hat, linen shirt, muzzle-loading rifle, team of oxen and one-bottomed plow, something like the minuteman statue in Lexington-Concord, Massachusetts. Like the western cowboy, he stands larger than life, stereotyped in tough simplicity. Had his trials and tribulations not been exaggerated, the myth of the hero-farmer might have withered and died.

The hard reality is that the cowboy was a small player in a much larger story of how mining, railroad construction, Pacific shipping, and sod-buster farming settled the West.[6] Generally speaking, the open-range grazing of cattle for which the cowboys are best known contributed little to the nation's gross national product, and was restricted to the southern high plains between Texas and the railhead towns in Kansas and Oklahoma. The cowboys' great overland cattle drives lasted less than twenty-five years, from the 1870s to no later than the early 1890s. Much the same can be said for the hardscrabble, stone-hauling, ax-swinging hero-farmer, here dubbed the "eastern cowboy." In the West, the cowboy's natural enemies were outlaws and Indians. In the East, the Indians had been vanquished before much of the forest was cleared. So, in the final stage of mythmaking, the Yankee farmer fought not against Indians but against a perceived excess of stone.

A few eastern cowboys did exist, blowing up enormous boulders and building a few monumental walls. But most of the early American stone walls, those that once bounded countless pastures and tillage fields, were the logical, almost knee-jerk, response to the farmer's need to define his own territory and contain waste stone. Most stone walls have more in common with the mounds of ants than with the trials of a hardscrabble life or the excitement of the open range.

೧೧

THE FINAL MYTH IS THAT STONE WALLS WILL LAST FOREVER. They cannot. The fate of nearly every mineral crystal on earth is to dissolve, to be washed to the sea, and to be recycled back into rock or some other organic form. And the fate of every object raised above the level of the ocean floor is to fall back down. Mountains come and mountains go. Stone walls raised up must tumble back down. All stone walls *must* dissolve back to the soil, and thence to the sea.

***An old stone wall disintegrating back
into the soil in the author's backyard.***

Geochemists precisely measure geological time with
the steady decay of radioactive isotopes—uranium, lead,
rubidium, potassium, argon, carbon. But measuring time
and understanding it are not the same. I think that to understand how long time actually is, we must have physical
contact with the earth's crust. We must be able to *feel* our
way through time.

One night last spring I placed the palm of my hand on
a lumpy granite boulder on the derelict wall surrounding
my property. It was still warm because the heat of the day
had not yet left the massive stone. It was rough because the

quartz grains were raised higher than their less-resistant neighbors. As I was touching the stone, I felt a tiny seismic impulse, followed quickly by a faint, almost metallic clunk in the distance. Puzzled at first, I suddenly realized what had happened. A stone in the wall had shifted its position, falling down slightly, to the underlying stone. Perhaps a tree root had finally thrown the wall out of balance, or a mineral grain between two stones had given way to a century's worth of pressure, or the soil was shrinking back from the heaving of winter. Never before had I heard and felt the clunk and shock of stones moving in a wall.

Hearing, feeling, or simply knowing that stone walls are falling apart made me ponder the fact that even the oldest stone walls are quite young compared to how long Earth has existed.

❧

IN SPITE OF THEIR RELATIVE YOUTH, OLD STONE WALLS ARE ancient enough to help make the modern world more tranquil. They encourage us to slow down. Charles Fish, writing of his Vermont family farm, said:

> *Walking east along the edge of pasture and stream, I come to the big rock meadow where an abrupt outcropping provides a place to climb and picnic. Even to my mind as a boy, the rock suggests permanence or, as I will later think, an anchor binding the shifting surface of the farm to the earth's core.*[7]

Like old ledges, abandoned stone walls can anchor our "shifting" lives to something rock solid, something natural.

But unlike ledges, there is a human component to every stone wall.

When I place my hand on one of the sun-warmed stones of my wall, it's easy for me to conjure up an image of the farmer who placed the stone there: his trousers muddy from the knees down, his shoulders locked for strength, his arms toughened by a thousand liftings, and his bruised hands gripping the skull-size cobble. By touching it, I can bridge the separation between my "ruburban" present and his rural past, at least for the moment.

In every human brain, ancient or modern, is a mental package of instinctual feelings, something the psychologist Carl Jung deemed the "collective unconscious." One manifestation of this instinct is an affinity for stone, especially when it is weathered, as on a natural outcrop. Perhaps early mankind saw stone outcrops as material for a tool, a rock shelter for a home, a cliff for an ambush, a cairn to drive game, a place to escape, or a cache for hidden food. Later, human hands placed one stone above the other to form a hunting blind, to bank a fire, or to make a bench.

Loren Eisley, a literary paleontologist, said of our fascination with stone, even in the twentieth and twenty-first centuries:

> *I see an old, old shape bent to the fire while north winds blow, snow gathers, but the man worships in his own way ..., stirs fires, places a stone and goes on his own path down into the dark from which our kind emerged. Rough elements created him and he creates out of the selfsame need. Ask nothing more for there is nothing, no answer, none. A stone-*

caressing animal paused here, in a lost cen-
tury by a little fire. Say that I saw, and set a
stone, one more Neanderthal, in the vast dy-
ing of the evening sun.[8]

Knowing that human antiquity is part of something
as old as the Earth reminds us of the dimensions of time.
Stone walls hold time like a set of Russian dolls. The
smallest doll, the one farthest inside, contains the oldest
things in the universe, the elements. Outward dolls, in
succession, are the minerals composed of elements; the
stones composed of minerals; the wall composed of
stones; and the modern, weathered surface, which is a
blend of everything. All of this time is contained in every
stone ". . . whose coat of elemental brown a passing universe put on," as Emily Dickinson wrote. A stone pulled
from an authentic New England wall speaks, all at once,
of ancient seas, glacial mud, and the tip of a scythe being
broken during spring mowing a century ago.

ഇരു

COLONIAL FARMERS KNEW PRACTICALLY NOTHING ABOUT WHY
and how rocks formed deep within the Earth or how frost
heave and other natural processes brought them to the
surface. In fact, most farmers blamed the devil for the fieldstones of New England, which appeared as if by black
magic in seventeenth- and eighteenth-century fields.

Generally speaking, New Englanders banished Satan
from their psyches during the early to mid–nineteenth
century, during the Transcendentalist movement, when
Ralph Waldo Emerson, Henry David Thoreau, Margaret
Fuller, and Bronson Alcott were reshaping an intellectual
climate appropriate for a new nation defining its identity

as separate from that of Europe. They shifted the focus of explanations away from the spiritual domain to the natural world. In the process, Americans began to view their world more scientifically.

Although the stone walls of the Transcendentalist era have often been viewed in quasireligious terms, stone walls should be seen for what they are—landforms. This scientific approach to stone walls need not and does not undermine our appreciation of them. Science can only add to the pleasure that comes with greater understanding. As Walt Whitman wrote:

> *Exact science and its practical movements are no checks on the greatest poet but always his encouragement and support ...The sailor and traveler ... the anatomist, chemist, astronomer, geologist, phrenologist, spiritualist, mathematician, historian, and lexicographer are not poets, but they are the lawgivers of poets and their construction underlies the structure of every perfect poem ... there shall be love between the poet and the man of demonstrable science.*[9]

Henry David Thoreau said in what is arguably his most famous quote, "In wildness is the preservation of the world." Thoreau did not use the word "wilderness," a geographic place untouched by human hand, but "wildness," which connotes a condition in which nature has the winning hand. It is here, in the semantic gulf between the two words "wildness" and "wilderness," that stone walls become especially evocative.

The wilderness of New England was lost when the first humans arrived more than twelve thousand years ago, probably from Asia, across the Bering Strait. But the wildness of the place continues. Given enough time, wildness will reduce the greatest human efforts to rubble, then to soil, then to sediment, then to aqueous solutions, sending them back to the sea where they will be reconstituted, once again, into rock. Ashes to ashes. Dust to dust. These evocative phrases might more accurately include a middle phrase like "ashes to trees to ashes" or "dust to stones to dust."

During American settlement, there was collective joy in watching the wilderness disappear. When the last of the frontier had been explored, however, there was a feeling of national melancholy mitigated only slightly by the surge of industrialization, which translated the craving for open space into a craving for power. New England could no longer be a "wilderness." But, with industrialization, the joy of wildness began to return.

The value of wildness is both ancient and pervasive. In Exodus 20:25 it is written, "And if you make me an altar of stone, you shall not build it of hewn stones; for if you wield your tool upon it you profane it."[10] Natural stones are unprofaned. Each can be a personal wildness. The mortar-free fieldstone wall satisfies our need for the primitive and the civilized in one convenient package.

The architectural historian Simon Schama digs especially deep into the tension between wildness and civilization in *Landscape and Memory.* Throughout his book, he laments that Americans are more detached from their landscape than are Europeans, with their revered ruins of past civilizations. Curiously, he ends his magnificent discourse on architectural history not with a cathedral, but with the humble stone wall.

> *There are places woven within the boundaries*
> *of a modern metropolitan sprawl where the*
> *boundaries between past and present, wild*
> *and domestic, collapse altogether. Below the*
> *hilltop clearing where my house stands are*
> *drystone walls, the remains of a vanished*
> *world . . . From the midst of this suburban*
> *wilderness, in the hours before dawn, barely a*
> *fairway away from the inevitably manicured*
> *country club, coyotes howl at the moon, set-*
> *ting off a frantic shrieking from the flocks of*
> *wild turkey hidden in the covers. This is*
> *Thoreau's kind of suburb.*[11]

The stone walls of New England stand guard against a future that seems to be coming too quickly. They urge us to slow down and to recall the past.

Each stone fallen from a wall is a gift to the soil. Roots and moisture below the forest will eventually wedge the stones apart. Then the minerals within the fragments will dissolve, wash to the sea as salt, and leave behind nothing more than a yellowish-brown clay residue. Fallen stones, broken stones, rotten stones . . . all are symbols of organic redemption. Nature is busy, like Whitman's "noiseless patient spider" reclaiming her crust, reminding us that all of history is paradoxically as eternal and ephemeral as a simple stone wall.

APPENDIX
Geologic Timelines

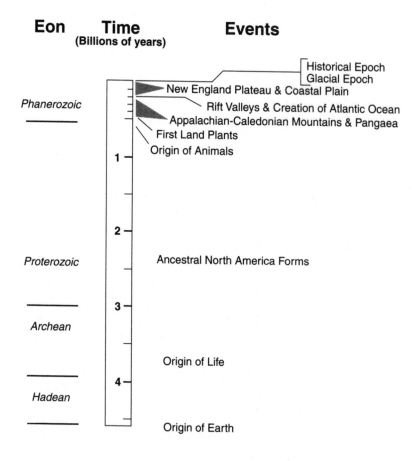

Eon   **Time**   **Events**
(Billions of years)

Historical Epoch
Glacial Epoch
New England Plateau & Coastal Plain

Phanerozoic
Rift Valleys & Creation of Atlantic Ocean
Appalachian-Caledonian Mountains & Pangaea
First Land Plants
Origin of Animals

1

2

Proterozoic   Ancestral North America Forms

3

Archean

Origin of Life

4

Hadean

Origin of Earth

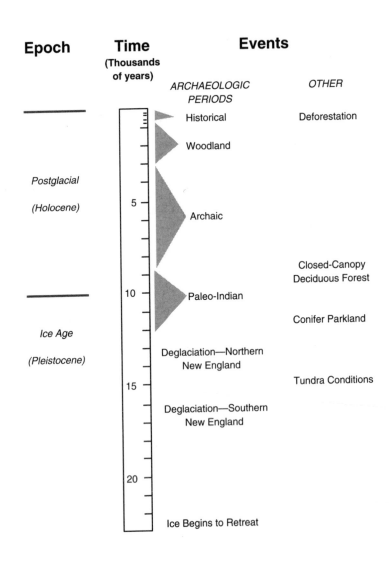

Historical Epoch	Time (Years A.D.)	Events
Environmental Awareness	**2000**	Present
Suburban Expansion		National Environmental Protection Act (1969)
Rural Rediscovery and Colonial Revival		Ford Motor Company Model T (1914)
	1900	
Abandonment of Upland Farms		Civil War (1861-1864)
		Erie Canal Completed (1820)
Rapid Interior Settlement and Intense Building of Stone Walls	**1800**	Revolutionary War (1776–1781)
		Treaty of Paris (1763)
Colonial Towns; Generally Coastal	**1700**	King Phillips War (1693)
Early Plantations		Massachusetts Bay Colony (1630) Plymouth Colony (Pilgrims; 1620)
	1600	North Virginia Company (1607)
Coastal Exploration		Coastal Fishing Stations

NOTES

∽

INTRODUCTION

1. Oliver Bowles, in *The Stone Industries* (New York: McGraw-Hill Book Company, Inc., 1939), estimated a total length of 246,000 miles in the United States, only a small portion of which lies outside the northeastern United States. For data, he used the U.S. Department of Agriculture Report "Statistics of Fences in the United States," 1872. Although stone "fence" was subsumed by the category labeled "Other" in the agriculture report, most of this material is indeed stone fence. Susan Allport (1990) used the same data to arrive at an estimate of 252,539 miles of stone wall in New England and adjacent New York.

1. ENGLAND AND NEW ENGLAND, COMMON GROUND

1. Howard Russell, in *A Long, Deep Furrow* (Hanover, NH: University Press of New England, 1976), provides a detailed account of European exploration of the New England coast, beginning in 1524 with Giovanni de Verrazano, a Florentine explorer, and continuing with encampments associated with fishing, forestry, and wild game prior to the Maine settlement. The Sagadahoc settlement was established by the Virginia Trading Company.

2. For a global review of early Earth history consult William K. Hartmann and Ron Miller, *The History of Earth; an Illustrated Chronicle of an Evolving Planet* (New York: Workman Publishing). For a review of New England's geological history consult Chet Raymo and Maureen Raymo, *Written in Stone, A Geological and Natural History of the Northeastern United States* (Chester, CT: Globe Pequot Press, 1989). For those with a geological background, an ideal reference is A. P. Benneson's *Geological Highway Map, Northeastern Region* (Tulsa, OK: American Association of Petroleum Geologists, 1966).

3. William Bradford, "The History of Plymouth Plantation, 1638," in *The American Tradition in Literature*, vol. 2., 3rd ed., Richard Croom Beatty and E. Hudson Long, eds. (New York: W. W. Norton & Co.), p. 35.

4. For the geological origin of the New England plateau, consult Charles Denny, *Geomorphology of New England* (Washington, DC: U.S. Geological Survey Professional Paper 1208, 1982). It is not a plateau in the traditional sense with a flat top and steep escarpments. Rather, it is an irregular surface of low relief below resistant highlands—the most famous of which is Mount Monadnock, in southern New Hampshire—but above a network of entrenched streams.

2. MAKING THE STONE

1. The difference between rock and stone is elusive for many readers. Rock is the raw material in situ. Stone usually connotes either human handling or human use, although it can also be used to describe naturally produced fragments of rock larger than a cobble. In spite of this distinction, the terms "stone wall" and "rock wall" or "stony fields" or "rocky fields" are used interchangeably. The statement excludes sand and gravel—used primarily for concrete, bituminous aggregate, and fill—which is presently the most valuable mineral resource in much of New England.

2. George Denton and Terrence Hughes, *The Last Great Ice Sheets* (1981). At the glacial maximum, the Laurentide Ice Sheet, which covered New England, was confluent with a mountain-glacier complex in the western Cordillera, Greenland, and the Canadian Arctic islands. Between this confluent system and Europe was a continuous cover of pack ice on the ocean. For a review of the Laurentide Ice Sheet in the United States, consult David Mickelson, et al., "The Laurentide Ice Sheet," in *Late Quaternary Environments of the United States,* ed. Stephen C. Porter (Minneapolis, MN: University of Minnesota Press, 1983), chapter 1. For a review of New England's Laurentide Ice Sheet, see Byron Stone and Harold Borns, "Pleistocene glacial and Interglacial stratigraphy of New England, Long Island and adjacent Georges Bank and Gulf of Maine," in V. Sibrava et al., 1986. For local details, consult the appropriate state geological survey.

3. Timothy Dwight, *Travels in New-England and New-York,* vol. 3, B. M. Solomon, ed. (Cambridge, MA: Harvard University Press, 1969), p. 72.

4. For a review of the glacial landform and the origin of its nomenclature, consult J. K. Charlesworth, *The Quaternary Era; With Special Reference to Its Glaciation* (London: Edwin Arnold, LTD, 1957).

5. The term "ablation till," although in common usage, is technically incorrect because nearly all till was released from the ice by "ablation," a technical term for the loss of ice by melting, sublimation, and the generation of icebergs, which is also called calving. Lodgment till was physically smeared (or lodged) on the land by moving ice. Ablation till is more properly called meltout till, most of which melted out of basal layers of the glacier after it had stopped moving.

3. BURYING THE STONE

1. Reinald L. Cook, ed., *Ralph Waldo Emerson, Selected Prose and Poetry,* 2nd ed. (New York: Holt Rinehart and Winston,

1969), p. 483. This poem is titled "Wealth," indicating the central place of soil in the early American economy. Such "naturalistic" thinking is a hallmark of Transcendentalism. Its writers looked to nature for explanations of everyday occurrences.

2. Descriptions of early soils by: 1) Peter Kalm, *Travels into North America*, trans. John Reinhold Forster and F.A.S. Warrington, in *The America of 1750, Peter Kalm's Travels in North America, The English Version of 1770*, ed. Adolph E. Benson (New York: Wilson-Ericson, Inc., 1937), p. 308. Note: The area(s) he is describing are not specifically mentioned, but the process is the same throughout the northeastern woodlands, regardless of whether they were north of the glacial border or not. 2) Timothy Dwight, *Travels in New-England and New-York*, p. 72.

3. For a review of early vegetation, refer to Thompson Webb, et al., "Vegetation, Lake Levels, and Climate in Eastern North America for the past 18,000 years," in *Global Climates since the last Glacial Maximum* (Minneapolis: University of Minnesota Press, 1993), H. E. Wright, et al. For a review of postglacial eolian conditions consult Robert M. Thorson and Carol Anne Schile, "Deglacial Eolian Regimes in New England," *Geological Society of America Bulletin* 107 (1995): 751–761.

4. Insights into the forest processes and diversity encountered by the colonists are found in: 1) David Foster and J. F. O'Keefe, *New England Forests Through Time; Insights from the Harvard Forest Dioramas* (Cambridge, MA: Harvard University Press, 2000); 2) Michael Williams, *Americans and Their Forests* (Cambridge, U.K.: Cambridge University Press, 1989); 3) William Cronon, *Changes in the Land; Indians, Colonists, and the Ecology of New England* (New York: Hill and Wang, 1983); 4) Gordon G. Whitney, *From Coastal Wilderness to Fruited Plain; A History of Environmental Change in Temperate North America from 1500 to the Present* (Cambridge, U.K: Cambridge University Press, 1994).

5. Dean Snow, *The Archaeology of New England* (New York: Academic Press, 1980), provides a review of the limited use of stone by Native Americans prior to European settlement.

6. John Stilgoe, *Common Landscape of America, 1580-1845* (New Haven, CT: Yale University Press, 1982), p. 143.

7. Samuel Deane, *The New England Farmer: Or Georgical Dictionary* (Worcester, MA: Isaiah Thomas, 1790), p. 306; the quote immediately following is from John Evelyn, *The Terra: A Philosophical Discourse of Earth,* 4th ed. (York, U.K.: Wilson and Son, 1662), p. 3 in 1821 reprinting.

8. In detail, the processes happening within soils are among the most complex in nature because soils represent the intersection of biology, meteorology, and geology. Recent technical reviews appropriate for the processes operating in northeastern soils include: 1) K. A. Armson, *Forest Soils: Properties and Processes* (Toronto: University of Toronto Press, 1977); 2) S. Pal Arya, *Introduction to Micrometeorology* (New York: Academic Press, Inc., 1988), pp. 262-285; and 3) F. H. Boormann and G. E. Likens, *Pattern and Process in a Forested Ecosystem* (New York: Springer Verlag, 1981).

9. The familiar hydrologic cycle concerns what is called meteoric water. The longer hydrological cycle involves "connate water," which is trapped within sediments before it becomes involved with volcanic and metamorphic reactions. New England's metamorphic and sedimentary rock was once saturated with connate water.

10. For a review of this fractionation process, and the many others that disturb soils and move stones around, consult Raymond Wood and Donald L. Johnson, "A Survey of Disturbance Processes and Archaeological Site Formation," *Advances in Archaeological Method and Theory* 1 (1988): 315-381.

11. Nathaniel Shaler, "The Origin and Nature of Soils," in U.S. Geological Survey, 12th Annual Report, 1890-1891, p. 280. The subsequent quote is from Walter Lyford, *Importance of*

ants to brown podzolic soil genesis in New England (Petersham, MA: Harvard Forest Paper No. 7, 1963).

12. P. A. Thomas and B. S. Robinson, *The John's Bridge Site; VT-FR-69: An Early Archaic Period Site in Northwestern Vermont* (Burlington, VT: University of Vermont, Department of Anthropology Report #28).

13. For specific details of these "stone-raising" processes, refer to: 1) H. J. Lutz, "Movements of rocks by uprootings of forest trees," *American Journal of Science* 258 (1960): 752; 2) Stephen Spur, "Forest Associations in the Harvard Forest," *Ecological Monographs* 26 (1956): 245–262. The subsequent reference to "spongy" soils is from David Foster and J. F. O'Keefe, *New England Forests Through Time: Insights from the Harvard Forest Dioramas* (Cambridge, MA: Harvard University Press, 2000), p. 25.

14. Although seemingly straightforward, "sea level" is neither level nor stationary, even when the effects of tides, waves, and storms are disregarded. Owing to differences in the strength in the Earth's gravitational field, there is about five hundred feet of relief on the topography of the surface ocean. Additionally, the sea surface rises and falls as its temperature changes and as water is taken from or returned to the atmosphere, glaciers, and groundwater. For a recent review of sea level off the coast of New England, refer to Thomas K. Weddle and Michael J. Retelle, *Deglacial History and Relative Sea-Level Changes, Northern New England and Adjacent Canada* (Boulder, CO: Geological Society of American Special Paper 351).

4. Taking the Forest

1. Quote from Howard Russell, *A Long Deep Furrow: Three Centuries of Farming in New England* (Hanover, NH: University Press of New England, 1976), p. 9. Text in the succeeding paragraphs is abstracted from his summary of early agricultural techniques.

2. Quotes in this paragraph are from John Hart, *The Rural*

Landscape (1998), p. 142. The quote in the next paragraph is from Walter Blair, Theodore Hornberger, and Steward Randall, *The Literature of the United States,* revised single vol. ed. (Glenview, IL: Scott Foresman and Company, 1957), p. 71.

3. James O. Robertson, *American Myth, American Reality* (New York: Hill and Wang, 1980, pp. 143-144), provides an excellent summary of the stages in the settlement process. Like Native Americans, frontiersmen also trod lightly on the landscape, leaving few, if any, stone walls. Walls resulted from people planning to stay put.

4. Paul Waggoner, written communication, January 2002.

5. Wolfgang Mieder, *A Dictionary of American Proverbs* (Oxford, U.K.: Oxford University Press, 1991). See also Clifton Fadiman, *The Little Brown Book of Anecdotes* (Boston: Little Brown, 1985), p. 302.

6. Peter N. Carroll, *Puritanism and the Wilderness; the Intellectual Significance of the New England Frontier, 1629-1700* (New York: Columbia University Press, 1969), p. 17. See also Roderick Nash, *Wilderness and the American Mind* (New Haven: Yale University Press, 1967).

7. All quotes in this paragraph from David Foster and J. F. O'Keefe, *New England Forests Through Time: Insights from the Harvard Forest Dioramas* (Cambridge, MA: Harvard University Press, 2000), p. 4. This book provides a dense, well-written synopsis of the changes that would have taken place elsewhere on the New England plateau.

8. Ibid., p. 6.

9. The first quote in this paragraph is from Ian G. Simmons, *Changing the Face of the Earth: Culture, Environment, History* (Cambridge, MA: Basil Blackwell, Inc., 1989), p. 166. The second quote is from Timothy Dwight, *Travels in New-England and New-York,* vol. 2 (Cambridge, MA: Harvard Univ. Press, 1821), pp. 2321-2324.

10. This Associated Press story was published in the *Hartford Courant* (Monday, June 11, 2001, page 1) citing archaeo-

logical research by Gerald Sawyer, City University of New
York, and Warren Perry, Central Connecticut State University.

11. Timothy Dwight, *Travels in New-England and New-York*
(Cambridge, MA: Harvard University Press, 1821), p. 465.
The quote in the next paragraph is from Jeremy Belknap,
The History of New Hampshire, vol. III (Boston: Belknap
and Young, 1792), p. 192.

12. Alfred Staebner, *Farming as a Way of Life* (Mansfield, CT:
Mansfield Historical Society, 1977), pp. 10-11.

13. More specifically, picket fences, as architectural ornamental
enclosures for house and garden, were, with a few unknown
exceptions, not used for fields. Whether this happened or
not will not be known, because all early fences have since
rotted away. Each farm must have had its own particular
style of fencing and history of fencing, because modern expedient fences in New England are made from whatever is
available, from rotted firewood to hay bales to brush thick-
ets. An early review of fences in early America was published by Wilbur Zelinsky, "Walls and Fences," *Landscape:
Magazine of Human Geography* 8:3 (1959): 14-21.

14. Quotes in this paragraph are from: 1) Michael Bell, "Did
New England Go Downhill?," *American Geographical
Review* 79 (1989): 450-456; 2) William Cronon, *Changes in
the Land, Indians, Colonists, and Ecology in New England*
(New York: Hill and Wang, 1983), p. 120; 3) Robert Sanford,
Don Huffer, and Nina Huffer, *Stone Walls and Cellarholes: A
Guide for Landowners on Historic Features and
Landscapes in Vermont's Forests*, 1995 rev. (Montpelier, VT:
Vermont Agency of Natural Resources, Department of
Forests, Parks, and Recreation), p. 10.

5. COPIOUS STONE

1. Paul Waggoner, *Farming Among the Stones*, written communication, January 2002. Geological factors played a critical role in this widespread distribution on the landscape.
After the best soils of coastal and large-river lowlands were

taken, the best available soils came in two spots: the tops of drumlins where the lodgment till was thick, and thousands of small interval lands in small river valleys. Additionally, good sites for small mills were spaced out along countless small streams, like beads on a string, being located only where the rock was strong.

2. Robert Gordon (2001) provides an excellent review of the early iron industry and its impact on regional forests. The controlled burning under the conditions of reduced oxygen, required to make charcoal, mimics that of when nature makes real coal. Gases and volatiles are driven off, increasing the purity of the carbon fuel, which means it burns at a higher temperature.

3. C. A. Federer, L. D. Flynn, C. W. Martin, J. W. Hornbeck, and R. S. Pierce, *Thirty Years of Hydrometeorologic Data at the Hubbard Brook Experimental Forest, New Hampshire* (U.S. Department of Agriculture Forest Service, Northeastern Forest Experiment Station, General Technical Report NE-141, 1990). They did not report the depth of freezing below lawns; that was obtained from my own observations while living in Hanover, New Hampshire, during the winter of 1992.

4. Samuel Deane, *The New England Farmer: Or Georgical Dictionary* (Worcester, MA: Isaiah Thomas, 1790), p. 110.

5. William Ruddiman, *Earth's Climate; Past and Future* (New York: W. H. Freeman and Company, 2001), provides a contemporary review of the little Ice Age. See also H. H. Lamb, *Climate and History* (New York: Metheun, 1985), for the earliest climatic data sets, including one assembled by Helmut Landsburg in 1968 on monthly temperatures in New England. Recent work associated with global warming and collected by the National Climatic Data Center support these findings.

6. Nathaniel Shaler, *The Origin and Nature of Soils* (U.S. Geological Survey 12th Annual Report, 1890–1891), pp. 213–345.

7. The summary of frost heaving is based on: 1) Laboratory data from Edwin J. Chamberlain, *Frost Susceptibility of Soil* (Washington, DC: U.S. Army Corps of Engineers Cold Regions Research and Engineering Laboratory Monograph 81-2); 2) Geological observations by Susan Prestrud-Anderson's "The Upfreezing Process," *Geological Society of America Bulletin* 100 (1988): 609-621; 3) Laboratory experiments by David B. Thorud and D. A. Anderson, "Freezing in Forest Soil as Influenced by Properties, Litter, and Snow," *University of Minnesota Water Resources Research Center Bulletin* 10 (1969); 4) Field data by G. R. Benoit and S. Mostaghimi, "Modeling Soil Frost Depth Under Three Tillage Systems," *Transactions of the American Society of Agricultural Engineers* 28 (1985): 1,499-1,505; 5) Engineering algorithms by George W. Aitken and R. L. Berg, *Digital Solution of Modified Berggren Equation to Calculate Depths of Freeze or Thaw in Multilayered Systems* (Hanover, NH: U.S. Army Corps of Engineers Cold Region Research and Engineering Laboratory Special Report 122, 1968).

8. This pattern was well documented by Stephen Spur, "Forest Associations in the Harvard Forest," *Ecological Monographs* 26 (1956): 245-262.

9. Connecticut Board of Agriculture, Session on Improvement of Rocky, Sandy, and Barren Land (Hartford: *Sixth Annual Report of the Secretary of the Connecticut Board of Agriculture*, 1872), pp. 116-148. This report also provides an interesting commentary on how "professional" farmers interacted to exchange ideas for mutual benefit.

10. Louis Agassiz, "The Ice Period in America," *Atlantic Monthly* 14 (1864): 86-93. This is a popular review of his investigations of North American glaciation. He was the principal author of the theory of ice ages, which he developed in Europe prior to being recruited to America by Harvard University.

11. Runoff by overland flow is actually very rare in forest soils

of the northeastern United States. What normally happens is that rainfall and snowmelt infiltrate easily through the tough network of roots until they encounter the impervious lodgment till or bedrock below, at which point the water flows laterally through macropores in a downhill direction at a level that is well above the regional water table. This is called subsurface storm flow.

12. Robert M. Thorson, et al., "Colonial Impacts to Wetlands in Lebanon, Connecticut," *Geological Society of America Reviews in Engineering Geology*, vol. XII (1998): 23–42. More specifically, consider the presettlement soil as an original mixture of coarse resistant elements (stones) and fine-grained elements (stream-carried mud and sand) that were segregated by the overland flow runoff processes.

13. Peter Kalm, *Travels into North America*, trans. John Reinhold Forster and F. A. S. Warrington. *The America of 1750, Peter Kalm's Travels in North America, The English Version of 1770*, ed. Adolph B. Benson (New York: Wilson-Ericson, Inc., 1937), p. 307.

14. David Foster, *Thoreau's Country* (Cambridge, MA: Harvard University Press, 1998), p. 60.

15. Timothy Dwight, *Travels in New-England and New-York* (Cambridge, MA: Harvard University Press, 1821), p. 267.

16. The wording of this quote is reported differently. This version is from page 19 of Eric Sloane's America. See also Michael Bell, *Face of Connecticut: Geology and the Land* (Hartford, CT: Connecticut Geology and Natural History Survey of Connecticut, Bulletin 110, 1985, p. 60) and Elijah Allen, *Cornwall in 1801* (Cornwall Historical Society, Cornwall, Connecticut, 1985).

17. David Foster, op. cit., p. 60.

18. John R. Stilgoe, *Common Landscape of America, 1580-1845* (New Haven: Yale University Press, 1982), p. XXX. Quote by Huntington from Milne, 1986.

19. The journal entry dated July 12, 1852, as reproduced by David Foster, op. cit., p. 60.

20. Susan Allport's *Sermons in Stone* (New York: W. W. Norton
    & Co., 1990), p. 121, compares the "lace walls" of Martha's
    Vineyard and the Galloway Dyke, a type of British wall, em-
    phasizing the open construction of both. The Galloway
    Dyke, as illustrated by Lawrence Garner, *Dry Stone Walls*
    (Buckinghamshire, U.K.: Shire Publications, Ltd., 1984), con-
    sists of a closely packed basal segment overlain by a veneer
    of rounded stones to intimidate climbing by sheep.

6. BUILDING WALLS

1. Streams with little sand and gravel in these open reaches do
    not have the aquifer capacity to buffer strong flows of wa-
    ter. In such settings, streams flow rapidly during and shortly
    after precipitation events, but are dry at other times. It is the
    unique combination of glacial action and bedrock geology
    that created perfect settings for mills.
2. Howard Russell, *A Long, Deep Furrow* (Hanover, NH:
    University Press of New England, 1976), provides a very ex-
    tensive review of this subject, and is the source of specific
    facts cited here.
3. Cited by Paul Johnson (1998), pp. 391–392. See also Hugh
    Raup's "The View From John Sanderson's Farm; A Perspec-
    tive for the Use of the Land," *Forest History* 10:1 (1966):
    1–11, which provides an example of how this interval of
    prosperity influenced farmsteads.
4. The calculation provides only a rough estimate for the work
    of assembling walls rather than hauling stone to the work
    site. Many assumptions are required. Chief among them is
    the use of an eight-hour day, the validity of the estimate for
    total wall length, and the average rate of construction.
5. In 1871, the average New England farm was 107 acres in
    size. If square, it would have had a perimeter of 7,662 feet,
    just more than a mile around. A calculation is possible if we
    assume that half the fence was wall, the walls were built on
    its perimeter, and the stones were hauled from the outer
    fifth of the area and were stacked thigh high 25 stones per

yard. Assuming realistic walking speeds of just less than 3 miles per hour, and allowing 5 seconds to lift a rock off the ground, it would take an average 3 minutes and 12 seconds to haul one rock to the edge. Each human conveyor belt would build just less than 1 yard per hour, or about 20 feet per day. An average-size man weighing 154 pounds burned 400 calories per hour doing pick-and-shovel work and 350 per hour walking on a horizontal surface at 3 miles per hour, carrying a 43-pound load.

6. William Cronon, *Changes in the Land* (New York: Hill and Wang, 1983), pp. 120–121, estimated thirty-five cords per year. This can be visualized as the annual firewood needs for a colonial family as a stack of wood four feet deep, four feet high, and three hundred feet long. According to Ester Morn Swift, the archivist at Vermont's Billings Museum, a topnotch woodcutter could cut up to three cords during a dawn-to-dusk day; the less expert farmer probably produced about a cord. This work—felling, limbing, sawing, splitting, and stacking—consumes energy at about 450 calories per hour. Assuming that wood was cut at the rate of two cords per day at a rate of 375 calories per hour.

7. Jeff Hawkins, the assistant football coach of the Dartmouth squad, provided these data in November 1991. More specifically, the mass of a player, when multiplied by the metabolic effort of each activity (calisthenics, playing, bench time, etc.), when integrated over the schedule for the season, yields the caloric output for an individual. Team output is simply the sum of its individuals, allowing for those who drop out.

8. In general, the methods used to construct a wall are self-evident. For a good primer on wall construction, present and past, refer to Kevin Gardner, *The Granite Kiss* (Woodstock, VT: Countryman, W. W. Norton Press, 2001). He expands on an even more succinct review by Susan Allport, op. cit.

9. An excellent summary of the changing protocols for the marking of survey boundaries prior to the mid–twentieth

century is contained within the U.S. Department of the Interior, Bureau of Land Management, Instructions for the Survey of Public Lands of the U.S. (Washington, DC: U.S. Government Printing Office, 1947).

10. For a visual comparison between British and American walls, consult Lawrence Garner, op. cit., and Allen Mac-Weeney and Richard Conniff, *Irish Walls* (New York: Tabori and Chang, 1986). Greater attention to architecture and fencing, respectively, are indicated for these walls relative to their New England counterparts.

11. John Warner Barber, *Connecticut Historical Connections* (New Haven, CT: B. L. Hamlen, 1838).

12. U.S. Department of Agriculture, Statistics of Fences in the United States, Report of the Commissioner of Agriculture for the Year 1871 (Washington, DC: U.S. Government Printing Office, 1872), pp. 497–512.

13. Letter from George Washington to John Sinclair dated December 11, 1796, as cited by Lyman Carrier, *The Beginnings of Agriculture in America* (New York: McGraw-Hill, Inc., 1923).

14. Quantitatively, the Pierson's correlation coefficient for non-New England farms was 0.89, a value that includes the data point of Pennsylvania. The value for the same coefficient for the New England states (0.54) is not significant.

15. Even when stone was "good and plenty," building a rod of stone wall (sixteen feet) cost thirteen shillings and two pence; this was two and a half times the cost of a post-and-rail fence, which cost only five shillings and three pence at the time. Curiously, the cost of building a hybrid fence was lowest of all, only three shillings and three pence, being 38 percent cheaper than one made solely of wood. The hybrid fence with three, instead of four, rails was cheaper because the stone eliminated the need for postholes in the soil, where they would rot, and because it required one fewer rail. Essentially, it was cheapest to place the fence on stone that was already there. In this case, the hybrid fence wasn't

a stone fence raised higher with wood, but a wooden fence actually built where a line of stone already existed. In most cases, the line of stone was, a generation or two earlier, nucleated by a wooden fence. Data contained within an unpublished report by John Treadwell, former governor of Connecticut, written between 1830 and 1845. Available at the Connecticut Academy of Arts and Sciences.

16. Quotation from John Seelye, *Yankee Drover, Being the Unpretending Life of Asa Sheldon, Farmer, Trader, and Working Man, 1788-1870* (Hanover, NH: University Press of New England, 1988), p. 140. Seelye's book introduces, annotates, and reproduces Sheldon's autobiography, which illustrates quite well the variety of skills many farmers maintained.

17. G. H. Ashley, "Studies in Appalachian Mountain Sculpture," *Geological Society of America Bulletin* 46 (1935): 1395-1436.

18. William Least-Heat Moon, *Blue Highways* (New York: Little Brown and Co., Atlantic Monthly Press Book, 1985), p. 307.

19. John Stilgoe, *Common Landscape of America, 1580-1845* (New Haven, CT: Yale University Press, 1982), p. 175. This paragraph inspired me to quantify the geometric relationships involved in the processes of wall construction.

20. As with all numerical models, the results depend on the assumptions that are made. I used a wall that was 1.0 meters at the base, 0.75 meters high, fields with a concentration of stone ranging from 1 to 3 percent by area, and a density of stone of 2.7 grams per cubic centimeter. Data for the length of the plow train was provided by Ester Morn Swift, archivist of the Vermont Billings Museum in December 1992, with her permission.

21. These maps were made available by Gordon Whitney of Harvard Forest. To make the calculation, I selected a discrete block consisting of multiple farms, measured the size of all enclosures bounded on three or more sides by a stone wall or a road, and determined the probabilities using statistical software.

22. Connecticut Board of Agriculture, *Sixth Annual Report of the Secretary of the Connecticut Board of Agriculture,* Session on Improvement of Rocky, Sandy, and Barren Land (Hartford, CT: Case, Lockwood and Company, 1872), p. 116. Mr. Platt specified single (tossed) walls, which he identified with the word "fence."

23. Journal entry dated February 20, 1842, as reproduced by David Foster, op. cit., p. 65.

24. These relationships are a direct outgrowth of the Pythagorean theorem. The gravity analogy is based on robust geographic and economic theories used by the delivery industry and by marketing departments.

25. U.S. Department of Health and Human Services, *Work Practices Guide for Manual Lifting* (Washington, DC.: U.S. Department of Commerce, National Technical Information Service, Technical Report 81–122, NIOSH 00115739, 1981).

7. LAND ABANDONED

1. Unpublished document by John Treadwell, former governor of Connecticut, written sometime between 1830 and 1845.

2. Howard Russell, op. cit., p. 427.

3. Robert Clifton, *Prongs, Points, and Stickers; A Complete and Illustrated Catalogue of Antique Barbed Wire* (Norman, OK: University of Oklahoma Press, 1973).

4. Elizabeth Forbes Morison, and Elting E. Morison, *New Hampshire; A Bicentennial History* (New York: W. W. Norton & Co., 1976), p. 137.

5. Paul Johnson, *A History of the American People* (New York: HarperCollins, 1998), p. 515.

6. Quoted from Bill McKibben, *The End of Nature* (New York: Doubleday, 1990), p. 5.

7. Technically, entropy is a measure of the waste heat produced in irreversible transformations. In common usage, it is a qualitative measure of the disorder of any self-contained system.

8. John Winthrop, *An Account of the Earthquake felt in*

New England, and the Neighbouring parts of America, on the 18th of November 1755, In a Letter to Tho. Birch (Cambridge, MA: Philosophical Transactions of the Royal Society [Great Britain], 1757).

9. Quoted by Russell Wheeler, Nathaniel K. Trevor, Archur C. Tarr, and Anthony Crone, *Earthquakes In and Near the Northeastern United States, 1638–1998* (U.S. Geological Survey Investigation Series I-2737, courtesy of the trustees of the Boston Public Library).

10. Edward C. Lathem, ed., *The Poetry of Robert Frost* (New York: Henry Holt and Co., 1979), p. 33. I suspect that "gaps" this wide were actually created by trees, either growing below or falling against the wall. Frost heaving usually dumps only a few stones.

11. The ubiquity and magnitude of walls as landforms was estimated by the mining engineer Oliver Bowles in his 1939 book, *The Stone Industries.* For data, he used the U.S. Department of Agriculture Report "Statistics of Fences in the United States," 1872. Although stone "fence" was subsumed by the category labeled "Other" in the report, most of this material is stone fences. This length of fencing is greater than the distance to the moon at its perigee, when it is closest to the Earth.

8. RURAL REVIVAL

1. These initial paragraphs present facts originally published by Howard Russell, *A Long, Deep Furrow* (Amherst, MA: University of Massachusetts Press, 1976).

2. Howard Mansfield, *In the Memory House* (Golden, CO: Fulcrum, 1993).

3. Roderick Nash, in *Wilderness and the American Mind* (New Haven, CT: Yale University Press, 1967), was the first to make explicit the American transition form loathing wilderness to loving it.

4. Harold Spencer, *Connecticut and American Impressionism* (Old Lyme, CT: Lyme Historical Society, 1980), p. 49.

5. I cannot prove that Weir built these walls; they were, however, rebuilt into unusual forms prior to his death.

6. Professor Jere Daniell of Dartmouth College recommended that I look to Wallace Nutting as a source of systematic visual information. Edie Clark's "The Man Who Looked Back and Saw the Future," *Yankee Magazine* (September 1986): 110–112 and 172–181), provides a biographical sketch of this unusual man.

7. From his photographic collection it is clear that stone walls were common, but seldom used as fences, which were almost always the height of an average man's chest and made of wire or wood. Most stone walls were made of chunky and slabby stones with the top ones lying as flat as possible, and at the height of a man's thigh (only a few were higher than a man's waist or lower than his knees). In only two pictures had the stones been fitted together tightly enough to qualify as a laid wall. In only one case was dimension (quarried) stone used. Only one picture showed large capstones. Only one picture showed copestones. Piles or heaps of stone appeared only twice. Compound fences (meaning stone and something else) usually used wire, rather than wood, which was strung on posts adjacent to the wall rather than mounted above it. In half of these cases, the posts simply leaned against the wall, using it for support, whereas in the other half, the upright posts were dug into the ground.

8. J. Brinkerhoff Jackson, *The Necessity for Ruins* (New Haven: Yale University Press, 1980), p. 102.

9. Edward C. Lathem, ed., *The Poetry of Robert Frost* (New York: Henry Holt and Co., 1979), p. 173. The quote is from the poem "Star in a Stone Boat."

10. Ibid., p. 23.

11. Eric Sloane, *America* (New York: Promontory Press, 1982), p. 23.

12. Quoted in Bradley, et al., *The American Tradition in Literature,* third edition (New York: W. W. Norton & Co., 1967), p. 37.

9. BACK TO NATURE

1. Paraphrased from James Vance (see bibliography).
2. Multiple quotes in this paragraph: Hector St. John de Crèvecouer, *Sketches of Eighteenth Century America*, Henri L. Bourdin, Ralph H. Gabariel, and Stanley T. Williams, eds. (New Haven: Yale University Press, 1925), p. 128.
3. Simon Schama, *Landscape and Memory* (New York: Alfred A. Knopf, 1995), p. 578, quoted Thoreau from Robert L. Rothwell, *Henry David Thoreau: An American Landscape* (New York: Marlowe & Company, 1995), pp. 126-127.
4. William Cronon, "The Trouble with Wilderness," in *Uncommon Ground, Towards Reinventing Nature* (New York: W. W. Norton and Co., 1995).
5. Edwin O. Wilson, *Consilience: The Unity of Knowledge* (New York: Alfred A. Knopf, 1998), p. 278.
6. Donald Worster, "The Vulnerable Earth: Toward a Planetary History," *The Ends of the Earth, Perspectives on Modern Environmental History,* ed. Donald Worster (New York: Cambridge University Press, 1990), p. 1,088. See also Paul Stern, "A second Environmental Science: Human-environment interactions," *Science* 260 (1993): 1897-1899; Carolyn Merchant, "Gender and Environmental History," *Journal of Environmental History* 76 (1990): 1117-1121; Steven Budiansky, *Nature's Keepers* (New York: The Free Press, 1995); Paul Colinvaux, "An Ecologist's View of History," *Yale Review* 64: 357-339.
7. Quote from editor's preface (unpaginated) in Curtis Fields, *The Forgotten Art of Building a Stone Wall* (Dublin, NH: Yankee Publishing Inc., 1971).
8. Noel Perrin, "Forever Virgin: The American View of America," Halpern, Daniel, *On Nature* (San Francisco: North Point Press, 1987), p. 15.
9. The farmer clearly provided the mechanical energy and decided where to put each stone, but may have done so as what the biologist E. O. Wilson describes, in *On Human Nature* (Cambridge, MA: Harvard University Press, 1978), p. 67, as "an

autonomous decision-making instrument, an alert scanner of the environment that approaches certain kinds of choices and not others." What this means is that the farmer may have built the wall without volition, almost absentmindedly.

10. WRIT IN STONE

1. Gordon Hayward, *Stone in the Garden: Inspiring Designs and Practical Projects* (New York: W. W. Norton & Co., 2001), p. 9.
2. Susan Allport, *Sermons in Stone* (New York: W. W. Norton & Co., 1990), p. 17.
3. Quoted in J. Ritchie Garrison, *Landscape and Material Life in Franklin County Massachusetts* (Knoxville, TN: University of Tennessee Press, 1991), taken from a Greenfield, Massachusetts, newspaper.
4. Elizabeth Forbes Morison, and Elting E. Morison, *New Hampshire: A Bicentennial History* (New York: W. W. Norton & Co., 1976).
5. Michael Bell, "Did New England Go Downhill," *American Geographical Review* 79 (1989): 450–456.
6. Richard White, *It's Your Misfortune and None of My Own: A New History of the American West* (Norman, OK: Oklahoma University Press, 1991).
7. Charles Fish, *In Good Hands, The Keeping of a Family Farm* (New York: Kodansha America Inc., 1995), p. 16.
8. Loren Eisley, *Innocent Assassins* (New York: Macmillan, 1973), p. 50.
9. Preface to Walt Whitman, *Leaves of Grass,* in *The American Tradition in Literature,* third edition, Sculley Bradley, Richmond Croom Beatty, and E. Hudson Long, eds. (W. W. Norton & Co., 1967), p. 27.
10. Exodus 20:25 quoted by M. Scott Peck, *In Search of Stones: A Pilgrimage of Faith, Reason, and Discovery* (New York: Hyperion, 1995).
11. Simon Schama, *Landscape and Memory* (New York: Alfred A. Knopf, 1995), p. 557.

BIBLIOGRAPHY

Agassiz, Louis. "1864: The Ice Period in America." *Atlantic Monthly,* vol. 14, 86–93.

Aitken, George W., and Richard L. Berg. "Digital Solution of Modified Berggren Equation to Calculate Depths of Freeze or Thaw in Multilayered Systems." U.S. Army Corps of Engineers CRREL Special Report 122 (1968), Hanover, NH.

Allport, Susan. *Sermons in Stone: The Stone Walls of New England and New York.* New York: W. W. Norton & Co., 1990.

American Husbandry, Containing an account of the soil, climate, production, and agriculture of the British colonies in North-America and the West Indies, by an American, in two volumes. London: printed for J. Bew, in Pater-noster Row, 1775.

Ardrey, Robert. *The Territorial Imperative: A Personal Inquiry into the Animal Origins of Property and Nations.* New York: Atheneum, 1966.

Armson, K. A. *Forest Soils: Properties and Processes.* Toronto, Canada: University of Toronto Press, 1977.

Arya, S. Pal. *Introduction to Micrometeorology.* New York: Academic Press, Inc., 1988.

Ashley, G. H. "Studies in Appalachian Mountain Sculpture." *Geological Society of America Bulletin,* vol. 46 (1935): 1395–1436.

Atsuyuki, Okabe, Barry Boots, and Kokichi Sugihara. *Spatial Tessellations, Concepts and Applications of Voronoi Diagrams.* New York: John Wiley & Sons, 1992.

Barber, John Warner. *Connecticut Historical Collections.* New Haven, CT: B. L. Hamlen, 1838.

Belknap, Jeremy. *The History of New Hampshire,* vol. III. Boston: Belknap and Young, 1792.

Bell, Michael. "Did New England Go Downhill?" *American Geographical Review,* vol. 79 (1980): 450–456.

———. "The Face of Connecticut: People, Geology and the Land: State Geological and Natural History Survey of Connecticut," bulletin 110 (1985), Hartford, CT.

Bennison, A. P. Geological Highway Map, Northeastern Region: American Association of Petroleum Geologists, U.S. Geological Highway Map Series no. 10, Tulsa, Oklahoma.

Benoit, G. R., and S. Mostaghimi. "Modeling Soil Frost Depth Under Three Tillage Systems." *Transactions of the American Society of Agricultural Engineers,* vol. 28 (1985): 1,499–1,505.

Berry, Wendell. *The Gift of Good Land: Further Essays Cultural and Agricultural.* San Francisco: North Point Press, 1981.

———. *The Unsettling of America: Culture & Agriculture,* third ed. San Francisco: Sierra Club Books, 1996.

Bidwell, Percy Wells, and John I. Falconer. *History of Agriculture in the Northern United States, 1620–1860.* New York: Peter Smith; reprint, Carnegie Institution of Washington, pub. no. 358.

Blair, Walter, Theodore Hornberger, and Randall Steward. *The Literature of the United States,* revised single-vol. ed. Chicago: Scott Foresman and Company, 1957.

Bloss, Kathryn. *A Gathering of Days: Diary of a Young American Girl.* New York: Macmillan, 1979.

Borman, F. H., and G. E. Likens. *Pattern and Process in a Forested Ecosystem.* New York: Springer Verlag, 1981.

Bowles, Oliver. *The Stone Industries,* 2nd ed. New York: McGraw-Hill Book Company, Inc., 1939.

Bradley, Sculley, Richard Croom Beatty, and E. Hudson Long. *The*

American Tradition in Literature, 3rd ed. New York: W. W. Norton & Co., 1967.

Brown, Marley R. III. "A survey of Historical Archaeology in New England." In *New England Historical Archaeology. The Dublin Seminar for New England Folklife*, annual proceedings, ed. Peter Bemes 1977.

Budiansky, Stephen. *Nature's Keepers: The New Science of Nature Management*. New York: The Free Press, 1995.

Buel, Jesse. "The Farmer's Companion; or Essays on the Principles and Practice of American Husbandry: Boston, Marsh, Capen, Lyon, and Webb." In *Agricultural Reformer, Selections from his Writings*, ed. Harry J. Carman and Jesse Buell. New York: Columbia University Press, 1947.

Canup, John. *Out of the Wilderness: The Emergence of an American Identity in Colonial New England*. Middletown, CT: Wesleyan University Press, 1990.

Carrier, Lyman. *The Beginnings of Agriculture in America*. New York: McGraw-Hill, 1923.

Carroll, Peter N. *Puritanism and the Wilderness: The Intellectual Significance of the New England Frontier 1629-1700*. New York: Columbia University Press, 1969.

Chamberlain, Edwin J. *Frost Susceptibility of Soil*. U.S. Army Corps of Engineers CRREL monograph 81-2, 1981.

Charlesworth, J. K. *The Quaternary Era; With Special Reference to Its Glaciation*, vol. 2. London: Edward Arnold, Ltd., 1957.

Chase, Alston. *In a Dark Wood: The Fight Over Forests and the Rising Tyranny of Ecology*. Boston, MA: Houghton Mifflin Company, 1995.

Clark, Edie. "The Man Who Looked Back and Saw the Future." *Yankee Magazine* (September 1986): 110-112, 172-181.

Clifton, Robert T. *Barbs, Prongs, Points, and Stickers: A Complete and Illustrated Catalogue of Antique Barbed Wire*. Norman, OK: University of Oklahoma Press, 1973.

Cole, Luane. *Lyme, New Hampshire, Patterns and Pieces, 1761/1976*. Lyme Historians, Inc., ed. Canaan, NH: Phoenix Publishing, 1976.

Colinvaux, Paul. "An Ecologist's View of History." *Yale Review* vol. 64 (1975): 357–369.

Connecticut Board of Agriculture. Session on Improvement of rocky, sandy, and barren land. In *Sixth Annual Report of the Secretary of the Connecticut Board of Agriculture*, Hartford, CT: Case, Lockwood and Company, 1872.

Crosby, Alfred. "An Enthusiastic Second." *Journal of American History*, vol. 76, no. 4 (1990): 1,107–1,110.

Crèvecoeur de, Hector St. John. *Sketches of Eighteenth Century America, or More Letters from an American Farmer,* Henri L. Bourdin, Ralph H. Gabriel, and Stanley T. Williams, eds. New Haven, CT: Yale University Press, 1925.

Cronon, William. *Changes in the Land: Indians, Colonists, and the Ecology of New England.* New York: Hill and Wang, 1983.

———, ed., *Uncommon Ground: Toward Reinventing Nature.* New York: W. W. Norton and Company.

Danhof, Clarence H. *Change in Agriculture: The Northern United States, 1820–1870.* Cambridge, MA: Harvard University Press, 1969.

Daniels, Bruce C. *The Connecticut Town: Growth and Development 1635–1790.* Middletown, CT: Wesleyan University Press, 1979.

Deane, Samuel. *The New England Farmer: Or Georgical Dictionary.* Worcester, MA: Isaiah Thomas, 1790.

Deetz, James F. *In Small Things Forgotten.* New York: Doubleday, 1977.

———. "Material Culture and World View in Colonial Anglo-America." In *The Recovery of Meaning,* Mark P. Leone, and Parker B. Potter, Jr., eds. Washington, DC: Smithsonian Institution Press, 1988.

Denny, C. S. "Geomorphology of New England." U.S. Geological Survey, professional paper 1208, 1982.

Denton, George H., and Terrence J. Hughes, eds. *The Last Great Ice Sheets.* New York: John Wiley & Sons, 1981.

Dillard, Annie. *Teaching a Stone to Talk: Expeditions and Encounters.* New York: Harper & Row, 1982.

Dinwiddie, Peter, et al. "Old-Growth Forests of Southern New England, New York, and Pennsylvania." In *Eastern Old Growth Forests,* M. B. Davis, ed. Washington, DC: Island Press, 1996.

Drowne, William. *Compendium of Agriculture; or the Farmers guide, in the most essential parts of Husbandry and Gardening; Compiled from the Best American and European publications, and unwritten opinions of experienced cultivators.* Providence, RI: Field and Mason, 1824.

Dwight, Timothy. *Travels in New-England and New-York,* 4 vols. B. M. Solomon, ed. Cambridge, MA: Harvard University Press, 1969.

Eisely, Loren. *Innocent Assassins.* New York: Macmillan, 1973.

Eliot, Jared. *Essays upon Field-Husbandry in New England.* H. J. Carman and R. G. Tugwell, eds. New York: Columbia University Press, 1934.

Evelyn, John. *The Terra: A Philosophical Discourse of Earth,* 4th ed. York, U.K: Wilson & Son, 1812.

Fadiman, Clifton. *The Little Brown Book of Anecdotes.* Boston: Little Brown, 1985.

Federer, C. A., L. D. Flynn, C. W. Martin, J. W. Hornbeck, and R. S. Pierce. Thirty years of hydrometeorologic data at the Hubbard Brook Experimental Forest, New Hampshire. U.S. Department of Agriculture Forest Service, Northeastern Forest Experiment Station, General Technical Report NE-141, 1990.

Fields, Curtis P. *The Forgotten Art of Building a Stone Wall.* Dublin, NH: Yankee Publishing Inc., 1971.

Fish, Charles. *In Good Hands: The Keeping of a Family Farm.* New York: Kodansha America Inc., 1995.

Foerste, August F. "Fence Wall Geology." *American Geologist,* vol. 4 (1889): 376–371.

Foster, David. *Thoreau's Country: Journey Through a Transformed Landscape.* Cambridge, MA: Harvard University Press, 1999.

Foster, David R., and J. F. O'Keefe. *New England Forests Through*

Time: Insights from the Harvard Forest Dioramas. Cambridge, MA: Harvard University Press, 2000.

French, H. M. *The Periglacial Environment.* New York: Longman Group Limited, 1976.

Gardner, Kevin. *The Granite Kiss: Traditions and Techniques of Building New England Stone Walls.* Woodstock, VT: The Countryman Press, W. W. Norton & Co., 2001.

Garner, Lawrence. *Dry Stone Walls.* Buckinghamshire, U.K.: Shire Publications, Ltd., 1984.

Garrison, J. Ritchie. *Landscape and Material Life in Franklin County, Massachusetts, 1770-1860.* Knoxville, TN: University of Tennessee Press, 1991.

Goldthwait, James W. "A Town that has gone downhill." *Geographical Review,* vol. 17 (1927): 527-552.

Goodwin, Brian. *The Evolution of Complexity.* New York: Simon & Schuster, 1994.

Gordon, Robert. *A Landscape Transformed: The Ironmaking District of Salisbury, Connecticut.* New York: Oxford University Press, 2001.

Goudie, Andrew. *The Human Impact: Man's Role in Environmental Change.* Cambridge, MA: MIT Press, 1982.

Griffin, Donald R. *Animal Thinking.* Cambridge, MA: Harvard University Press, 1984.

Halpern, Daniel. *On Nature: Nature, Landscape, and Natural History.* San Francisco: North Point Press, 1987.

Happold, F. C. *Mysticism: A Study and an Anthology.* London: Penguin Books, 1988.

Hart, John F. *The Rural Landscape.* Baltimore: Johns Hopkins University Press, 1998.

Hartmann, William K., and Ron Miller. *The History of Earth: An Illustrated Chronicle of an Evolving Planet.* New York: Workman Publishing, 1991.

Hawkes, Jacquetta. *The Atlas of Early Man.* New York: St. Martin's Press, 1976, reprint 1996.

Hayward, Gordon. *Stone in the Garden: Inspiring Designs and Practical Projects.* New York: W. W. Norton & Co., 2001.

Hill, David E., E. H. Suetter, and Walter N. Gonick. "Soils of Connecticut," bulletin 787, Connecticut Agricultural Experiment Station, New Haven, 1980.

Holcombe, Harold G. "Stone Walls in Eastern Connecticut." *Antiquarian*, vol. 2 (1950): 24–31.

Hubka, Thomas C. *Big House, Little House, Back House, Barn: The Connected Farm Buildings of New England.* Hanover, NH: University Press of New England, 1984.

Hume, Ivor. *A Guide to Artifacts of Colonial America.* New York: Alfred A. Knopf, 1970.

Hunt, Charles B. *Surficial Deposits of the United States.* New York: Van Nostrand Reinhold, 1986.

Jackson, John B. *Discovering the Vernacular Landscape.* New Haven, CT: Yale University Press, 1984.

——. *The Necessity for Ruins, and Other Topics.* Amherst, MA: University of Massachusetts Press, 1980.

Johnson, Chris E., Arthur H. Johnson, Thomas G. Huntington, and Thomas G. Siccama. "Whole-Tree clearcutting effects on soil horizons and organic-matter pools." *Soil Science Society of America Journal,* vol. 55 (1991): 497–502.

Johnson, Donald L., and Kenneth L. Hansen. "The effects of frost-heaving on objects in soils." *Plains Anthropologist,* vol. 19, no. 64 (1974): 81–98.

Johnson, Paul. *A History of the American People.* New York: HarperCollins Publishers, 1998.

Jorgensen, Neil. *A Guide to New England's Landscape.* Chester, CT: The Globe Pequot Press, 1977.

Josselyn, John. "An account of two voyages to New-England, London." In *John Josselyn, Colonial Traveler, A Critical Edition of Two Voyages to New-England,* Paul J. Lindholt and John Josselyn, eds. Hanover, NH: University Press of New England, 1988

Kalm, Peter. *Travels into North America,* trans. John Reinhold Forster and F. A. S. Warrington. In *The America of 1750, Peter Kalm's Travels in North America, The English Version of 1770,* Adolph. B. Benson, ed. New York: Wilson-Ericson, Inc., 1937.

Kay, James J., and Eric Schneider. "Embracing Complexity: The Challenge of the Ecosystem Approach." *Alternatives,* vol. 20, no. 3 (1994): 32–39.

Kelly, Kevin. *Out of Control: The New Biology of Machines, Social Systems and the Economic World.* Reading, MA: Addison Wesley, 1994.

King, Marsha, K. "Archaeological survey and documentation of the stone walls adjacent to Stone Road, Daniels Mill Village, Killingly, Connecticut." Pawtucket, RI: Public Archaeology Laboratory, Inc., Report no. 213-1 (1988).

King, Phillip B., and Helen Beikman. "Geological Map of the United States." U.S. Geological Survey, professional paper 903, 1976.

Kirby, Jack T. "Gardening with J. Crew: The Political Economy of Restoration Ecology." *Beyond Preservation: Restoring and Inventing Landscapes,* A. Dwight Baldwin Jr., Judith De Luce, and Carl Pletsch, eds. Minneapolis, MN: University of Minnesota Press, 1994.

Kuperman, Karen Ordahl. *Captain John Smith: A Select Edition of His Writings.* Chapel Hill, NC: University of North Carolina Press, 1988.

Lamb, H. H. *Climatic History and the Future.* New York: Metheun, 1985.

Landsberg, H. E. "Two centuries of New England climate." *Weatherwise* (April 1967): 52–57.

Larkin, Jack. *The Reshaping of Everyday Life: 179-1840.* New York: HarperCollins, 1998.

Lathem, Edward C., ed. *The Poetry of Robert Frost.* New York: Henry Holt and Company, 1979.

Least-Heat Moon, William. *Blue Highways.* Boston: Little Brown and Co., 1985.

Leveson, David. *A Sense of the Earth.* Garden City, NJ: Anchor Natural History Books, 1972.

Lindgren, James M. *Preserving Historic New England; Preservation, Progressivism, and the Remaking of Memory.* New York: Oxford University Press, 1995.

Lutz, H. J. "Movement of rocks by uprootings of forest trees." *American Journal of Science,* vol. 258 (1960): 752.

Lyford, Walter H. "Importance of ants to brown podzolic soil genesis in New England." Petersham, MA: Harvard Forest paper no. 7, 1963.

MacWeeney, Allen, and Richard Conniff. *Irish Walls.* New York: Tabori and Chang, 1986.

McKibben, Bill. *The End of Nature.* New York: Doubleday, 1989.

Mansfield, Howard. *In the Memory House.* Golden, CO: Fulcrum, 1993.

Mavor, James W., Jr., and Byron E. Dix. *Manitou: The Sacred Landscape of New England's Native Civilization.* Rochester, VT: Inner Traditions International, 1989.

Marsh, George P. *Man and Nature: or, Physical Geography as Modified by Human Action.* New York: Charles Scribner, edited by David Lowenthal. Cambridge, MA: Harvard University Press, 1965.

Merchant, Carolyn. "Gender and Environmental History." *Journal of American History,* vol. 76, no. 4 (1990): 1,117–1,121.

Mickelson, David, et al. *The Laurentide Ice Sheet.* In *Late Quaternary Environments of the United States,* S. C. Porter, ed. Minneapolis, MN: University of Minnesota Press, 1983.

Mieder, Wolfgang, ed. *A Dictionary of American Proverbs.* New York: Oxford University Press, 1991.

Milne, George M. *Lebanon: Three Centuries in a Connecticut Hilltop Town.* Canaan, NH: Phoenix Publishing, 1986.

Mitchell, John H. *Living at the End of Time.* Boston: Houghton Mifflin Co., 1990.

Morison, Elizabeth Forbes, and Elting E. Morison. *New Hampshire; A Bicentennial History.* New York: W. W. Norton & Co., 1976.

Morton, Thomas. *New English Canaan.* Originally published in Amsterdam in 1637. *The New English Canaan of Thomas Morton,* with introductory matter and notes by Charles F. Adams Jr. Boston: The Prince Society, 1883.

Murray-Wooley, and Karl Raitz. *Rock Fences of the Bluegrass.* Lexington, KY: The University Press of Kentucky, 1992.

Nash, Roderick. *Wilderness and the American Mind.* New Haven, CT: Yale University Press, 1967.

Naveh, Zev, and Arthur S. Lieberman. *Landscape Ecology Theory and Application,* student edition. New York: Springer-Verlag, 1990.

Olson, Sigurd F. "The Spiritual Aspects of Wilderness." In *Wilderness: America's Living Heritage,* D. Brower, ed. San Francisco: Sierra Club Books, 1961.

Peck, M. Scott. *In Search of Stones: A Pilgrimage of Faith, Reason, and Discovery.* New York: Hyperion, 1995.

Perin, Noel. "Forever Virgin: The American View of America." *On Nature, Landscape, and Natural History,* David Halpern, ed. San Francisco: North Point Press, 1987.

Petroski, Henry. *The Evolution of Useful Things.* New York: Alfred A. Knopf, 1992.

Pettengill, Samuel B. *The Yankee Pioneers: A Saga of Courage.* Rutland, VT: Charles Tuttle Co., 1971.

Pewe, Troy L., Richard E. Church, and Marvin J. Andersen. "Origin and Paleoclimatic significance of large-scale patterned ground in the Donnelly Dome Area, Alaska." Geological Society of America special paper, no. 103, 1969.

Pirsig, Robert M. *Zen and the Art of Motorcycle Maintenance: Inquiry into Values.* New York: Bantam Books, 1974.

Prigonine, I. "Order through fluctuation: Self-organization and social system." In *Evolution and Consciousness: Human Systems in Transition,* E. Jantsch and C. W. Waddington, eds. Reading, MA: Addison Wesley, 1976.

Prothero, Donald R., and Robert H. Dott, Jr. *Evolution of the Earth,* 6th ed. New York: McGraw-Hill, 2002.

Prestrud-Anderson, Suzanne P. "The upfreezing process; experiments with a single clast." *Geological Society of America Bulletin* vol. 100 (1988): 609–621.

Pye, Kenneth. *Aeolian Dust and Dust Deposits.* New York: Academic Press, 1987.

Rainsford-Hannay, Colonel F. *Dry Stone Walling*, 3rd ed. Stewarty of Kirkcudbrightshire Drystane Dyking Committee.

Raup, H. M. "The view from John Sanderson's farm; a perspective for the use of the land." *Forest History*, vol. 10, no. 1 (1966): 1–11.

Raymo, Chet, and Maureen, E. Raymo. *Written in Stone: A Geological and Natural History of the Northeastern United States*. Chester, CT: The Globe Pequot Press, 1989.

Robertson, J. O. *American Myth, American Reality*. New York: Hill and Wang, 1980.

Ruddiman, William F. *Earth's Climate: Past and Future*. New York: W. H. Freeman, 2001.

Russell, Howard. *A Long, Deep Furrow: Three Centuries of Farming in New England*. Hanover, NH: University Press of New England, 1976.

Sanford, Robert, Don Huffer, and Nina Huffer. "Stone Walls and Cellarholes: A Guide for Landowners on Historic Features and Landscapes in Vermont's Forests." Vermont Agency of Natural Resources, Department of Forests, Parks, and Recreation, 1995 revision.

Schama, Simon. *Landscape and Memory*. New York: Alfred A. Knopf, 1995.

Seelye, John. *Yankee Drover, Being the Unpretending Life of Asa Sheldon, Farmer, Trader, and Working Man, 1788–1870*. Hanover, NH: University Press of New England, 1988.

Shaler, Nathaniel. S. "The origin and nature of soils." U.S. Geological Survey 12th Annual Report, 1890–1891.

Simmons, Ian. G. *Changing the Face of the Earth: Culture, Environment, History*. Cambridge, MA: Basil Blackwell, Inc. 1989.

Sloane, Eric. *Diary of an Early American Boy, Noah Blake 1805*. New York: Wilfred Funk, Inc., 1962.

Sloane, Eric. *Eric Sloane's America*. New York: Promontory Press, 1982.

Snow, Dean R. *The Archaeology of New England*. New York: Academic Press, 1980.

Spencer, Harold. *Connecticut and American Impressionism* (catalog). A Cooperative Exhibitions Project, William Benton Museum of Art, Storrs; Hurlbutt Gallery, Greenwich Library; Lyme Historical Society, Old Lyme, 1980.

Spur, Stephen. "Forest Associations in the Harvard Forest." *Ecological Monographs,* vol. 26 (1956): 245-262.

Staebner, Alfred. *Farming as a Way of Life.* Mansfield, CT: Mansfield Historical Society, 1977.

Stern, Paul C. "A second environmental science: Human-environment interactions." *Science,* vol. 260 (1993): 1,897-1,899.

Stevens, P. S. *Patterns in Nature.* Boston: Little, Brown and Company, 1974.

Stephens, E. P. "The uprooting of trees, a forest process." *Soil Science Society of America Proceedings,* vol. 20 (1956): 113-116.

Stilgoe, John R. *Common Landscape of America, 1580-1845.* New Haven, CT: Yale University Press, 1982.

Stone, Byron D., and H. W. Borns. "Pleistocene glacial and interglacial stratigraphy of New England, Long Island and adjacent Georges Bank and Gulf of Maine." In *Quaternary Glaciations in the Northern Hemisphere: Quaternary Science Reviews,* V. Sibrava, D. Q. Bowen, and G. M. Richmond, eds., vol. 5 (1986): 39-52.

Symon, J. A. *Scottish Farming, Past and Present.* Edinburgh, Scotland: Oliver and Boyd, 1959.

Tansley, Arthur G. "The Use and Abuse of Vegetational Concepts and Terms." *Ecology,* vol. 16 (1935): 292.

Thomas, P. A., and B. S. Robinson. "The John's Bridge Site: VT-FR-69: An Early Archaic Period Site in Northwestern Vermont." University of Vermont, Department of Anthropology, report no. 28, 1980.

Thoreau, Henry D. *Walden.* Boston: Houghton Mifflin Company, 1960.

Thornbury, William D. *Regional Geomorphology of the United States.* New York: John Wiley & Sons, 1965.

Thorson, R. M., Andrew G. Harris, S. L. Harris, Robert Gradie III, and M. W. Lefor. "Colonial impacts to wetlands in Lebanon, Connecticut." In *A Paradox of Power: Voices of Warning and Reason in the Geosciences,* C. W. W. Welby and M. E. Gowan, eds. Boulder, *Geological Society of America Reviews in Engineering Geology,* vol. XII (1998): 23-42.

Thorson, R. M., and C. A. Schile. "Deglacial Eolian Regimes in New England." *Geological Society of America Bulletin,* vol. 107 (1995): 751-761.

Thorud, David B., and David A. Anderson. "Freezing in forest soil as influenced by properties, litter, and snow." University of Minnesota, Water Resources Research Center, bulletin 10, 1969.

Tocqueville, Alexis de. *Journey to America.* J. P. Mayer, ed., p. 329. G. Lawrence, trans. Garden City, NY: Doubleday and Company, 1971.

Treadwell, John, unpublished manuscript in Treadwell Collection, Connecticut State Library, Hartford, CT.

Turekian, Karl K. *Global Environmental Change, Past, Present, and Future.* Upper Saddle River, NJ: Prentice Hall, 1996.

Turner, B. L., et al., eds. *The Earth as Transformed by Human Action; Global and Regional Changes in the Biosphere Over the Past 300 Years.* Cambridge, U.K.: Cambridge University Press, 1992.

Urban, Dean L., Robert V. O'Neill, and H. A. Shugart. "Landscape Ecology." *Bioscience,* vol. 37, no. 2 (1987): 119-127.

U.S. Department of Agriculture. "Statistics of Fences in the United States." In *Report of the Commissioner of Agriculture for the Year 1871.* Washington, DC: U.S. Government Printing Office, 1872.

―――. "Soil Conservation Service, Soil Survey. Staff," *Soil Taxonomy, Agricultural Handbook no. 436.* Washington, DC: U.S. Government Printing Office, 1975.

U.S. Department of Health and Human Services. "Work Practices Guide for Manual Lifting." U.S. Department of Commerce, National Technical Information Service, Technical Report 81-122, NIOSH 00115739, 1981.

U.S. Department of the Interior, Bureau of Land Management. *Instructions for the Survey of Public Lands of the U.S.* Washington, DC: U.S. Government Printing Office, 1947.

Van Divber, Bradford B. *Roadside Geology of Vermont and New Hampshire.* Missoula, Montana: Mountain Press Publishing Company, 1987.

Vance, James E., Jr. "Democratic utopia and the American landscape." In *The Making of the American Landscape,* Michael P. Conzen, ed. Boston: Unwin Hyman, 1990.

Vitaliano, Dorothy B. *Legends of the Earth: Their Geologic Origins.* Bloomington, IN: Indiana University Press, 1973.

Waggoner, Paul. written communication, January 2002, from the manuscript titled *Fertile Farms Among the Stones,* used with author's permission.

Washburn, A. L. *Geocryology: A Survey of Periglacial Processes and Environments.* New York: John Wiley & Sons, 1980.

————. "Near-surface soil displacement in sorted circles, Resolute area, Cornwallis Island, Canadian High Arctic." *Canadian Journal of Earth Science,* vol. 26 (1988): 941–955.

Webb, T., III, Patrick J. Bartlein, Sandy P. Harrison, and Katherine H. Anderson. "Vegetation, Lake Levels, and Climate in Eastern North America for the Past 18,000 Years." In *Global Climates Since the Last Glacial Maximum,* H. E. Wright, Jr., et al., eds. Minneapolis, MN: University of Minnesota Press, 1993.

Wessels, Tom. *Reading the Forested Landscape: A Natural History of New England.* Woodstock, VT: Countryman Press, 1999.

White, Richard. *It's Your Misfortune and None of My Own: A New History of the American West.* Norman, OK: Oklahoma University Press, 1991.

Whitman, Walt. *Leaves of Grass.* Sculley Bradley, Richmond Croom Beatty, and E. Hudson Long, eds., *The American Tradition in Literature,* vol. 2, 3rd ed. New York: Norton, 1967.

Whitney, Gordon, G. *From Coastal Wilderness to Fruited Plain: A History of Environmental Change in Temperate North America from 1500 to the Present.* Cambridge, England: Cambridge University Press, 1994.

Whitney, Peter. *The history of the county of Worcester, in the Commonwealth of Massachusetts: with a particular account of every town from its first settlement to the present time; including its ecclesiastical state, together with a geographical description of the same. To which is prefixed, a map of the country at large, from actual survey.* Worcester, MA: Isaiah Thomas, Printers, 1793.

Williams, Michael. *Americans and Their Forests.* Cambridge, U.K.: Cambridge University Press, 1989.

Wilson, Edward O. *Consilience: the Unity of Knowledge.* New York: Alfred A. Knopf, 1998.

——. *On Human Nature.* Cambridge MA: Harvard University Press, 1978.

Wilson, Harold Fisher. *The Hill Country of Northern New England; Its Social and Economic History 1790-1930,* Harry J. Carman and Rexford G. Tugwell, eds. New York: Columbia University Press, 1936.

Winthrop, John. "An Account of the Earthquake felt in New England, and the Neighbouring parts of America, on the 18th of November 1755, In a Letter to Tho. Birch, D.D. Secret, from Cambridge New England." Philosophical Transactions of the Royal Society (Great Britain), reprint *Northeastern Geology,* vol. 4, no. 2 (1982): 105-110.

Woldenberg, Michael J. "The Average Hexagon in Spatial Hierarchies." In *Spatial Analysis in Geomorphology,* Richard J. Chorley, ed. New York: Harper & Row, 1972.

Wood, J. S., and M. Steinitz. "A world we have gained: house, common, and village in New England." *Journal of Historical Geography,* vol. 18 (1992): 105-120.

Wood, Raymond, and Donald L. Johnson. "A survey of disturbance processes and archaeological site formation.

Advances in Archaeological Method and Theory, vol. 1 (1988): 315–381.

Wood, William. *New England's Prospect: A True, Lively, and Experimental Description, 1634.* Boston: Publications of the Prince Society, vol. 1, reprint 1865.

Worster, Donald. "The Vulnerable Earth: Toward a Planetary History." In *The Ends of the Earth: Perspectives on Modern Environmental History,* Donald Worster, ed. New York: Cambridge University Press, 1988.

————. "Transformations of the Earth: Toward an Agroecologial Perspective in History." *Journal of American History,* vol. 76 (1990): 1,087–1,110.

Wright, H. E., J. E. Kutzbach Jr., T. Webb III, W. F. Ruddiman, F. A. and Bartlein Strut-Perrott, eds. *Global Climates Since the Last Glacial Maximum.* Minneapolis: University of Minnesota Press, 1993.

Zelinsky, Wilbur. "Walls and Fences." *Landscape: Magazine of Human Geography,* vol. 8, no. 3 (1959): 14–20.

CREDITS

က

The images on the pages noted have been reproduced or adapted from the following sources.

Page 16:   *Earth: Portrait of a Planet* by Stephen Marshak.
                New York: W.W. Norton & Company, 2001.
Page 19:   *Evolution of the Earth*, 6th ed. by Donald R. Prothero
                and Robert H. Dott. New York: McGraw Hill, 2002.
Page 39:   *Written in Stone* by Chet Raymo and Maureen E.
                Raymo. Chester, CT: The Globe Pequot Press, 1989.
Page 44:   Cushings/Whitney Medical Library, Yale University.
Pages 76, 120: *A Long, Deep Furrow* by Howard Russell. Hanover,
                NH: University Press of New England, 1976.
Page 79:   "Democratic utopia and the American landscape" by
                James E. Vance Jr. *The Making of the American
                Landscape*, Michael P. Conzen, ed. Boston: Unwin
                Hyman, 1990.
Page 88:   The Fisher Museum, Petersham, Massachusetts.
Page 104:   *The Face of Connecticut, People, Geology, and the
                Land*, Bulletin 110. The State Geological and Natural
                History Survey of Connecticut.
Page 114:   Historic Coast and Geodetic Survey Collection, NOAA
                Central Library.
Page 122:   Billings Farm & Museum, Woodstock, VT.
Page 139:   The Chicago Historical Society.
Page 149:   *Connecticut Historical Collections* by John Warner
                Barber. New Haven, CT: B. L. Hamlen, 1838.
Page 160:   "Archaeological survey and documentation of the stone
                walls adjacent to Stone Road, Daniels Mill Village,
                Killington, Connecticut, by Marsha K. King.

273

INDEX

ဟ